Quilts from Quarters

Pam & Nicky Lintott

Quilts from Quarters

12 CLEVER QUILT PATTERNS TO MAKE FROM FAT OR LONG QUARTERS

QRP

QUILT ROOM PUBLICATIONS

Contents

Quilts from Quarters – long and fat

Since the publication of our book *Jelly Roll Quilts* in 2008 we have made many quilts using jelly rolls, layer cakes and charm packs, but we have never forgotten our first love – that irresistible bundle of fat quarters. It was the original pre-cut pack, which we loved then and we love now. Most quilters feel the same, and have at least a few fat quarters tucked away in their fabric stash.

However, jelly roll quilts require strips cut from the full width of the fabric so long quarters (quarter yards) are often bought when adding strips to a jelly roll quilt. This means that long quarters are now just as popular as fat quarters and we need to acknowledge that fact.

Most fabric stashes therefore are a mix of both fat quarters and long quarters, and sometimes it becomes difficult to decide upon a quilt design to use up your stash.

We thought long and hard about this and decided there should be quilt patterns which gave instructions for both fat quarters and long quarters. Often the instructions are not that dissimilar but we wanted to make the cutting instructions clear and foolproof so you would not be put off starting a quilt with a mix of both kinds of quarters.

The quilts in this book can be made using either fat quarters or long quarters, and our cutting instructions clearly show how to cut your fabric using either a fat or a long quarter. Even within the same quilt you can mix and match long and fat quarters. If we have added background fabric, our instructions use the width of the fabric at 42 inches.

So have fun – use up your fabric stash, mix and match long and fat – and we hope you enjoy making the quilts in this book.

Pam & Nicky

WHAT IS A FAT QUARTER?

Possibly the most popular pre-cut fabric size of all, the fat quarter starts life as a half yard or half metre cut across the width of a 42in bolt of fabric, which is then cut vertically in two. The result is a useful 'fat' rectangle of fabric.

■ A fat quarter yard measures 18 x 21in
■ A fat quarter metre measures approximately 19 x 21in
■ When writing the patterns for this book we have assumed that 18 x 21in is the usable amount of fabric you can get from your fat quarter.

WHAT IS A LONG QUARTER?

Also known as a quarter yard, a thin quarter or a skinny quarter, this pre-cut is a quarter yard or quarter metre cut across the width of a bolt of fabric. For continuity in this book we always call it a long quarter which is how we refer to it in the UK.

■ A long quarter yard measures 9 x 42in
■ A long quarter metre measures approximately 9½ x 42in
■ When writing the patterns for this book we have assumed 9 x 42in as the usable amount of fabric you can get from your long quarter.

The Quilts

Simple Stars

A super simple quilt embellished with a little appliqué – just the project to get you started. We used a quick and easy technique for making the half-square triangles and a quick method for the appliqué using iron-on interfacing. We chose four bright quarters from the Dashwood Twist range set against a crisp white background.

This quilt uses the Twist range from Dashwood Studio. It was made by the authors and quilted by The Quilt Room.

Preparation

YOU WILL NEED

- Four quarters
- 1½yd (1.3m) background fabric
- ½yd (40cm) binding fabric
- ½yd (50cm) iron-on interfacing

FAT QUARTER CUTTING INSTRUCTIONS
Cut each of the four fat quarters as follows:

- Two strips measuring 6⅞in x 21in. Sub-cut each of these into three 6⅞in squares to make a total of six 6⅞in squares in all four colours.
- Set the excess fabric aside to make the appliqué leaves.

LONG QUARTER CUTTING INSTRUCTIONS
Cut each of the four long quarters as follows:

- One strip measuring 6⅞in x 42in. Sub-cut into six 6⅞in squares to make a total of six 6⅞in squares in all four colours.
- Set the excess fabric aside to make the appliqué leaves.

CUTTING THE OTHER FABRICS

Background fabric

- Cut four 6⅞in strips across the width of the fabric and sub-cut each strip into six 6⅞in squares to make a total of twenty-four 6⅞in squares.
- Cut three 6½in strips across the width of the fabric and sub-cut each strip into six 6½in squares to make a total of eighteen 6½in background squares. You need sixteen, so two are spare.

Binding fabric

- Cut five 2½in strips across the width of the fabric.

FINISHED SIZE: 48 x 48in (122 x 122cm)

BLOCK SIZE: 24in

Making the Quilt

HALF-SQUARE TRIANGLE UNITS

1 Mark across the diagonal on the reverse of all twenty-four 6⅞in background squares (fig 1).

2 Lay one marked 6⅞in background square on top of a 6⅞in square cut from a fat or long quarter, right sides together, making sure the edges are aligned (fig 2). Pin in position.

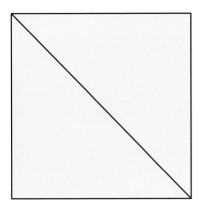

FIG 1

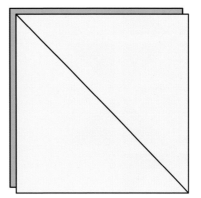

FIG 2

3 Sew a scant ¼in seam allowance either side of the marked line (fig 3).

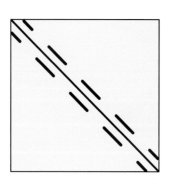 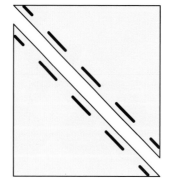

FIG 3

4 Cut along the marked diagonal line. Press open (towards the darker fabric) to create two half-square triangle units (fig 4). Repeat with all twenty-four 6⅞in squares and twenty-four 6⅞in background squares to make a total of forty-eight half-square triangle units. Keep the units from each colour together.

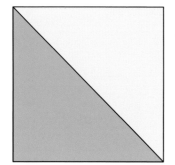 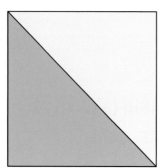

FIG 4

PUTTING THE STARS TOGETHER

5 Working with the half-square triangles in one colourway, sew the units together with four 6½in background squares, firstly into rows and then sew the rows together, to make one block (fig 5). Press the seams of alternate rows in opposite directions so the seams nest together nicely and pin at all

intersections to ensure a perfect match.
Repeat with the half-square triangle units from the other three quarters to make four blocks (fig 6).

FIG 6

6 Sew the four blocks together, pinning at all seam intersections to ensure a perfect match (fig 7).

FIG 7

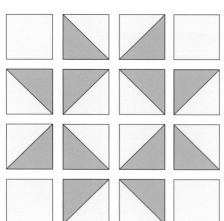

FIG 5

MAKING THE APPLIQUÉ LEAVES

7 Trace the leaf template (see page 112) on to iron-on interfacing and cut out the shape roughly – do not cut out exactly at this stage.

8 Lay the rough fusible side of the interfacing shape on to the right side of the fabric.

9 Reduce your stitch length and sew all around the shape on the drawn line and then trim the interfacing and the fabric to less than ¼in from the stitching line.

10 Cut a slit in the interfacing large enough to enable you to turn the interfacing carefully to the wrong side of your fabric.

11 Push out the seams and finger press into shape. Iron the leaf into position on your quilt. Hand or machine sew around the edge to secure the shape in place.

12 Repeat with all twenty-four leaves, ironing them in place and then hand or machine sewing to secure them in position.

13 Your quilt top is now complete. Quilt as desired and bind to finish (see *General Techniques*).

Freestyle Fancy

This is certainly a quilt in a dash – you'll have the quilt top finished in no time at all! The beauty of this design is how liberated you can be with it. Feel free to use our instructions as a base but mix it up and create your own unique quilt. This design is especially well suited to fabrics you really want to show off.

This quilt uses the collection Rise, by Melody Miller of Ruby Star Society for Moda. It was made by the authors and quilted by The Quilt Room.

Preparation

YOU WILL NEED
- Eleven quarters
- ⅝yd (50cm) binding fabric

FAT AND LONG QUARTER CUTTING INSTRUCTIONS
Cut each of the eleven quarters in half to make two 9 x 21in width rectangles.

CUTTING THE OTHER FABRICS
Binding fabric
Cut seven 2½in strips across the width of the fabric.

FINISHED SIZE: 51 x 73in (130 x 187cm)

Making the Quilt

CREATING THE UNITS

1 Choose two 9 x 21in rectangles and cut each into strips. We cut ours into five strips each – one 6½ x 9in, three 3½ x 9in and then the remainder in equal sized widths (fig 1). You can cut the strips in different widths for variety if you like. Sew together, alternating them to make two striped rectangles approximately 9 x 19in (fig 2). Press.

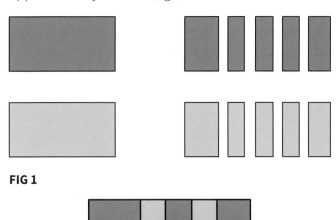

FIG 1

FIG 2

2 Repeat with another pair of 9 x 21in rectangles so you have two more striped rectangles approx. 9 x 19in (figs 3 & 4). Press.

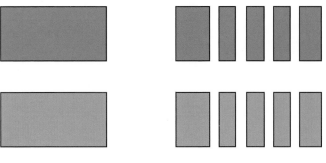

FIG 3

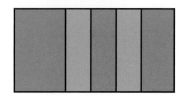

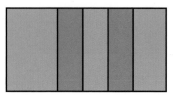

FIG 4

ASSEMBLING THE LENGTHS

3 Now take the remaining eighteen 9 x 21in rectangles and sew them into a continuous length, inserting the striped rectangles at four separate points, as shown (fig 5). Press.

FIG 5

4 Measure the continuous length of the rectangles. Divide this by six and then cut six equal lengths (fig 6). We cut six lengths of 73in (187cm).

FIG 6

5 When you are happy with how the lengths look next to each other (fig 7), sew them together (see layout on page 18). Press your seams open.

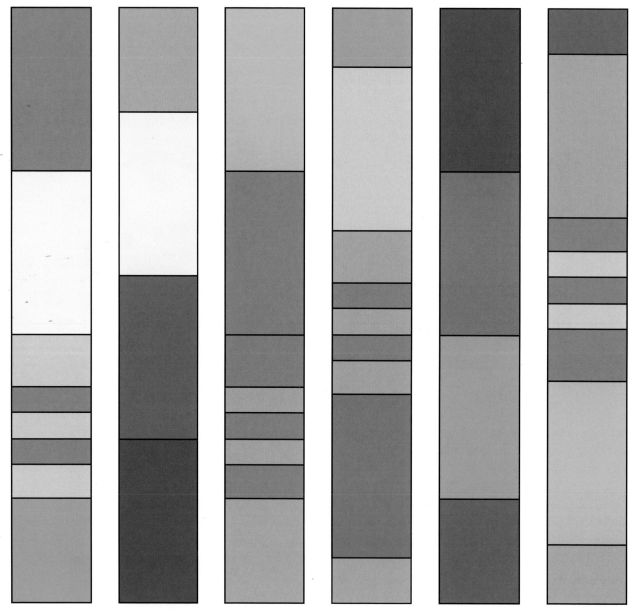

FIG 7

6 Your quilt top is now complete. Quilt as desired and bind to finish (see *General Techniques*).

Freestyle Fancy 21

Square Deal

When fabrics are as gorgeous as Kaffe Fassett's you really want to let them to do the talking. This is a quick and easy quilt to sew and it shows off the fabrics to their best advantage. We couldn't resist making this quilt in two colourways – hot and cool – and both look gorgeous. See our 'cool' quilt on page 4.

This quilt uses a collection from the Kaffe Fassett Collective. It was made by the authors and quilted by The Quilt Room.

Preparation

YOU WILL NEED
- Twelve quarters
- 2½yd (2.25m) background fabric
- ⅝yd (50cm) binding fabric

FAT QUARTER CUTTING INSTRUCTIONS
- Choose four quarters to make the large squares and from each of these quarters cut four 7½in squares to make a total of sixteen 7½in squares.
- From seven of the remaining eight quarters cut three 4½ x 21in strips and sub-cut each strip into four 4½in squares to make eighty-four.
- From the last quarter cut four 4½ x 21in strips and sub-cut each into four 4½in squares. *If you are working with fat quarter yards this is tight so take care when cutting.* You now have one hundred 4½in squares.

LONG QUARTER CUTTING INSTRUCTIONS
- Choose four quarters to make the large squares and from each of these cut one 7½ x 42in strip. Sub-cut into four 7½in squares to make a total of sixteen 7½in squares.
- From the remaining eight quarters cut two 4½ x 42in strips and sub-cut each into eight 4½in squares. You need one hundred 4½in squares.

CUTTING THE OTHER FABRICS
Background fabric
- Cut twenty-eight 1½in strips across the width of the fabric.
- Take six strips and sub-cut each strip into nine 1½ x 4½in rectangles to make a total of fifty 1½ x 4½in rectangles (with four spare).
- Take seven strips and sub-cut each strip into five 1½ x 7½in rectangles to make a total of thirty-two 1½ x 7½in rectangles (with three spare).
- Take fifteen strips and sub-cut each strip into four 1½ x 9½in rectangles to make a total of fifty-seven 1½ x 9½in rectangles (with three spare).
- Cut two 14½in strips across the width of the fabric and sub-cut into four 14½in squares. Cut across both diagonals of each 14½in square to make a total of sixteen setting triangles (fig 1).

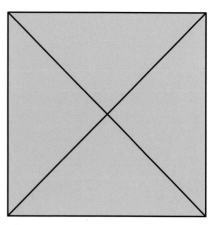

FIG 1

■ Cut one 8½in strip across the width of the fabric and sub-cut into two 8½in squares. Cut across one diagonal of each square to make four corner triangles (fig 2).

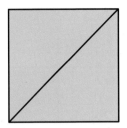

FIG 2

TIP Cutting the setting and corner triangles in the way we have suggested ensures that there are no bias edges on the outside of your quilt.

Binding fabric
■ Cut seven 2½in strips across the width of the fabric.

FINISHED SIZE: 64 x 64in (163 x 163cm)
BLOCK SIZE: 9in

Making the Quilt

CREATING BLOCK A

1 Sew a 1½ x 7½in background rectangle to both sides of a 7½in square and press as shown by the arrows (fig 3).

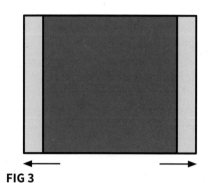

FIG 3

2 Sew a 1½ x 9½in rectangle to the top and bottom of the unit and press as shown by the arrows. Repeat to make sixteen of **Block A** (fig 4).

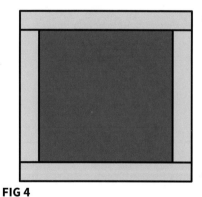

FIG 4

3 CREATING BLOCK B

4 Take two 4½in squares and a 1½ x 4½in background rectangle, sew together and press as shown (fig 5). Repeat with another two 4½in squares and a 1½ x 4½in background rectangle.

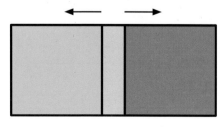

FIG 5

5 Sew the two units together with a 1½ x 9½in background rectangle in between and press (fig 6).

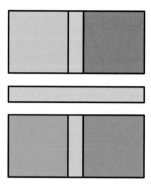

FIG 6

6 Repeat to make twenty-five **Block B** (fig 7).

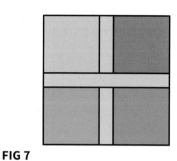

FIG 7

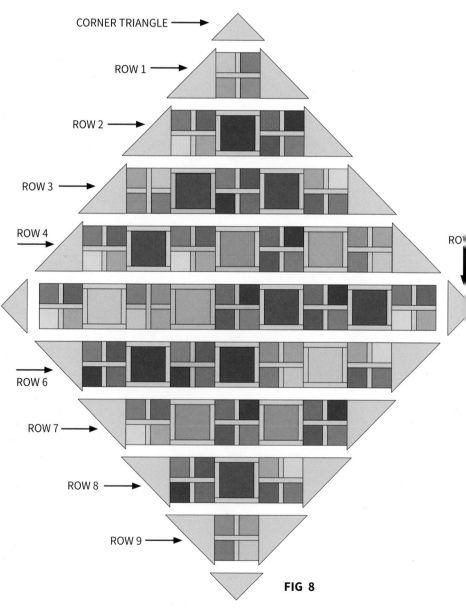

CORNER TRIANGLE

ROW 1

ROW 2

ROW 3

ROW 4

RO

ROW 6

ROW 7

ROW 8

ROW 9

FIG 8

ASSEMBLING THE QUILT

7 Referring to fig 8, lay out your blocks in rows, starting row 1 with Block B. When you are happy with the arrangement, sew the blocks into rows with a setting triangle at both ends. Don't sew the corner triangles on yet. Note that the setting triangles are cut slightly larger to make the blocks 'float', so when sewing these on make sure the bottom of the triangle is aligned with the bottom of the block (fig 9).

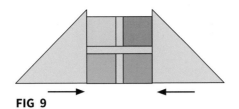

FIG 9

8 Sew the rows together pinning at every intersection to ensure a perfect match.

9 Your quilt top is now complete. Quilt as desired and bind to finish (see *General Techniques*).

Hearts and Crosses

Showcase some bright, bold fabrics that you love in this heart-themed quilt, with neat little crosses set on point. It could be the perfect design to make as a gift for someone who is leaving home, or just needs a bit of TLC, or if you *really* love those fabrics you'd better just keep it for yourself!

This quilt uses the collection Bright Eyes by Anna Maria Horner for FreeSpirit Fabrics. It was made by the authors and quilted by The Quilt Room.

Preparation

YOU WILL NEED
- Eighteen quarters
- 4½yd (4.25m) background fabric
- Scrappy binding made from the excess fabric (see tip on page 34)

SORTING THE FABRICS
Choose nine quarters for the top sections of the heart block and nine for the lower sections. Six of the quarters used in the top sections of the heart block will also be used in the cross blocks.

LONG QUARTER CUTTING INSTRUCTIONS
- From each of the nine long quarters for the top section of the heart, cut one 4½ x 42in strip and sub-cut four 4½ x 6½in rectangles to make a total of thirty-six rectangles. You need thirty-four so two are spare.
- From six of these quarters cut one 1½ x 42in strip. Sub-cut each of the six strips into three 1½ x 3½in rectangles and one 1½ x 10½in rectangle. Set these aside to use in the cross blocks.
- From each of the nine long quarters for the lower section of the heart, cut one 8½ x 42in strip and sub-cut each into two 8½ x 12½in rectangles. You need seventeen so one is spare.

FAT QUARTER CUTTING INSTRUCTIONS
- From each of the nine fat quarters for the top section of the hearts, cut two 4½ x 21in strips and sub-cut four 4½ x 6½in rectangles from each strip to make a total of thirty-six rectangles. You need thirty-four so two are spare.

TIP If your fabric is non-directional you could cut one 6½in x 21in strip but for directional fabric cut two 4½in strips.

- From six of these quarters cut one 1½ x 21in strip. Sub-cut each of the six strips into three 1½ x 3½in rectangles and set these aside together with the remainder of the strip (approx 10½in) to use in the cross blocks.
- From each of the nine fat quarters for the lower section of the hearts, cut two 8½ x 21in strips and sub-cut each into two 8½ x 12½in rectangles. You need seventeen so one is spare.

CUTTING THE OTHER FABRICS
Background fabric for the heart block
- Cut six 6½ x 42in strips and sub-cut each strip into six 6½in squares. You need thirty-four so two are spare.

- Cut five 2½ x 42in strips and sub-cut each strip into sixteen 2½in squares. You need sixty-eight 2½in squares so twelve are spare.

Background fabric for the cross block
- Cut three 1½ x 42in strips and sub-cut into a total of twelve 1½ x 10½in rectangles.
- Cut two 4¼ x 42in strips and sub-cut into a total of eighteen 4¼in squares.
- Cut across both diagonals of each 4¼in square to make seventy-two quarter-square triangles (fig 1).

FIG 1

- Cut seventeen 4½ x 42in strips and sub-cut twelve strips into thirty-six 4½ x 12¾in rectangles, and five strips into thirty-six 4½ x 4¾in rectangles.

Background fabric for the border
- Cut eight 2½in wide strips across the width of the fabric (42in).

FINISHED SIZE: 64 x 88in (163 x 224cm)

BLOCK SIZE: 12in

Making the Quilt

CREATING THE HEART BLOCK

1 With right sides together, lay one 2½in background square on one of the 4½ x 6½in rectangles for the top section (fig 2). Sew across the diagonal. You may like to draw the diagonal line to mark your stitching line or mark the diagonal with a fold.

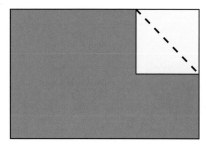

FIG 2

2 Flip the square over and press towards the background fabric (fig 3). Once you can see that the corner has been sewn on accurately, trim the excess fabric.

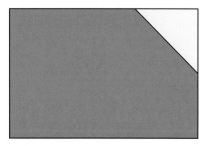

FIG 3

3 Take a second 2½in background square and lay it on the other side as shown and sew across the diagonal as before. Flip the square over, press and trim the excess fabric (fig 4).

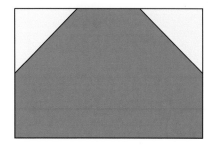

FIG 4

4 Repeat to make a second unit in the same fabric and sew them together as shown (fig 5), pinning at the seam intersection to ensure a perfect match. Press.

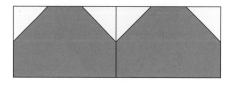

FIG 5

5 With right sides together, lay one 6½in background square on one of the 8½ x 12½in rectangles for the lower section as shown (fig 6). Sew across the diagonal. You may like to draw the diagonal line first to mark your stitching line or mark the diagonal with a fold.

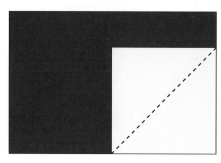

FIG 6

6 Flip the square over and press towards the outside of the block. If you have drawn a parallel line (see tip), cut between the sewn lines and set the half-square triangle units aside. If you have not drawn a parallel line, trim the excess fabric. Repeat on the second corner (fig 8). Press.

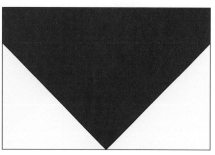

FIG 8

7 Sew the top and lower section of the heart together and press (fig 9). This block now measures 12½ x 12½in. Repeat to make seventeen heart blocks.

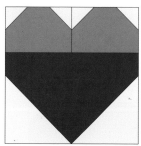

FIG 9

TIP This is not an integral part of the quilt but with just a little extra work you end up with ready-sewn half-square triangle units which can be used in another project – so no fabric wastage! Sew a parallel line ½in from the diagonal line as shown and then cut between the two sewn lines (fig 7).

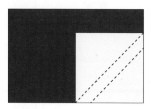 

FIG 7

CREATING THE CROSS BLOCK

8 Sew two 1½ x 10½in background strips and one 1½in strip allocated for the cross blocks together as shown (fig 10). Press to the darker fabric. Repeat to make six strip units.

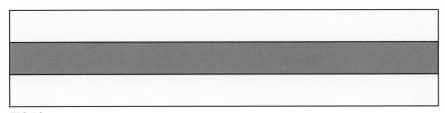

FIG 10

9 Cut each strip unit into six 1½in segments to make a total of thirty-six segments (fig 11).

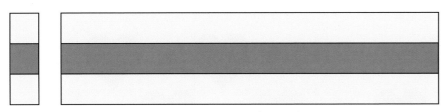

FIG 11

10 Take two segments and a 1½ x 3½in rectangle of the same fabric and sew together as shown (fig 12). Press the seams towards the centre rectangle.

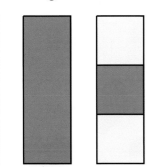

FIG 12

11 Make eighteen of these units. They measure 3½in square (fig 13).

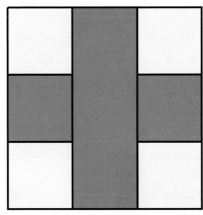

FIG 13

12 Sew the background quarter-square triangles and press (fig 14). These units should measure 4¾ x 4¾in. Repeat to make a total of eighteen.

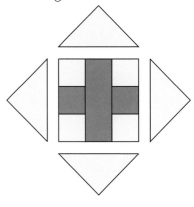

FIG 14

13 Sew two 4½ x 4¾in background rectangles to both sides of the unit, and sew two 4½ x 12¾in rectangles to the top and bottom (fig 15). Press.

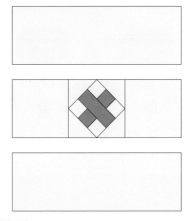

FIG 15

14 This will make a 12¾in square. Trim to measure 12½ x 12½in (fig 16).

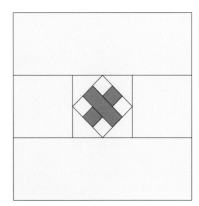

FIG 16

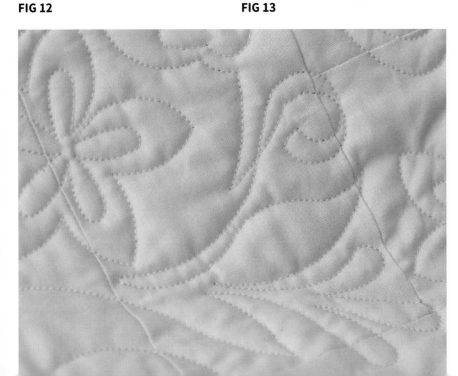

ASSEMBLING THE QUILT

15 Lay out the blocks, alternating the hearts with the crosses (fig 17). When you are happy with the arrangement, sew the blocks into rows, pressing the seams towards the heart blocks, as shown by the arrows. Sew the rows together pinning at all seam intersections to ensure a perfect match.

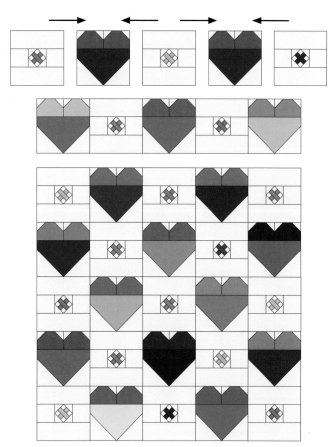

FIG 17

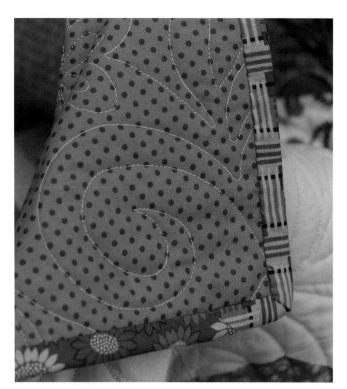

ADDING THE BORDERS

16 Sew the eight border strips into a continuous length of fabric.
17 Determine the vertical measurement from top to bottom through the centre of your quilt top. Cut two side borders to this measurement. Pin and sew to the quilt, easing if necessary (fig 18).
18 Determine the horizontal measurement from side to side across the centre of the quilt top. Cut two border strips to this measurement. Pin and sew to the top and bottom of the quilt (fig 18). Press towards the border fabric.
19 Your quilt top is now complete. Quilt as desired and bind to finish (see *General Techniques*).

FIG 18

TIP To make a scrappy binding, cut 2½in strips from the excess fabric and sew into a continuous length of approximately 320in.

Colour Play

This is a simple block to sew, but time needs to be spent on selecting the colours used. Our aim was to create a design which showed the changing of colours when one fabric was apparently laid over the top of another. Even if you can't achieve this appearance of transparency, this design still looks good so don't fret too much about the effect.

This quilt uses fabrics selected from Tula Pink's Designer Solids. It was made by the authors and quilted by The Quilt Room.

Preparation

YOU WILL NEED
- Twenty quarters
- 2¾yd (2.5m) white background fabric for blocks, borders and binding

SORTING THE FABRICS
There are four different blocks and each block requires five fabrics plus background fabric.
- Fabrics 1 and 4 need to be darker.
- Fabric 5 is the colour of the square you are laying over the top of fabrics 1 and 4.
- Fabrics 2 and 3 are the colours created when 5 is laid over 1 and 4.

See photograph and list of fabrics used, on page 43, for guidance on the placement of colours.

FAT QUARTER CUTTING INSTRUCTIONS
- **Fabric 1:** Cut two 3½ x 21in strips and sub-cut into four 3½ x 6½in rectangles and four 3½in squares. Cut one 2½ x 21in strip and set aside for the pieced border.
- **Fabric 2:** Cut one 3½ x 21in strip and sub-cut one 3½in square. Trim the balance of the strip to measure 2½in wide and set aside for the pieced border.
- **Fabric 3:** Cut one 3½ x 21in strip and sub-cut one 3½in square. Trim the balance of the strip to measure 2½in wide and set aside for the pieced border.
- **Fabric 4:** Cut two 3½ x 21in strips and sub-cut into four 3½ x 6½in rectangles and four 3½in squares. Cut one 2½ x 21in strip and set aside for the pieced border.
- **Fabric 5:** Cut one 3½ x 21in strip and sub-cut two 3½in squares. Trim the balance of the strip to measure 2½in wide and set aside for the pieced border.

Designing a Transparency Quilt

There's no actual transparency in a transparency quilt – but you can create the illusion that you can see through a shape to the one below by clever choice of colours and by arranging the piecing to suggest that shapes overlap one another.

LONG QUARTER CUTTING INSTRUCTIONS
- Cut all the long quarters in half to make two 9 x 21in rectangles, then follow the instructions given for fat quarters.

CUTTING THE BACKGROUND FABRIC

■ Cut nine 3½ x 42in strips across the width of the fabric and sub-cut six strips into thirty-two 3½ x 6½in rectangles and three strips into thirty-two 3½in squares.

■ Take the rest of the fabric (approx 62in) and fold *lengthways*. Cut thirteen 2½ x 62in strips down the length of the fabric. Eight of these will need to be trimmed to size for the borders as follows (but we suggest checking your quilt top measurements first): two 2½ x 48½in, two 2½ x 52½in, two 2½ x 56½in and two 2½ x 60½in. Set the remaining five 2½ x 62in strips aside for the binding.

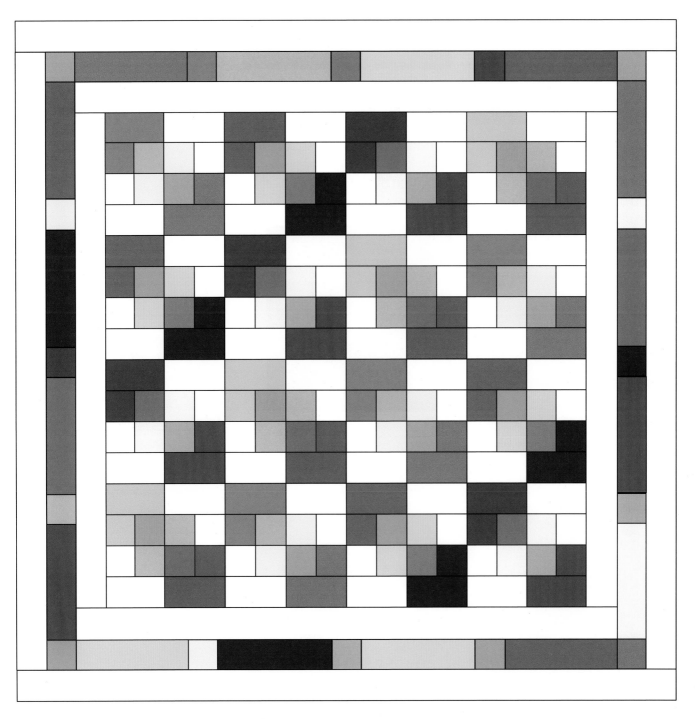

FINISHED SIZE: 60 x 60in (152 x 152cm)
BLOCK SIZE: 12in

Making the Quilt

CREATING THE UNITS

1 Working with one group of fabrics at a time, sew a fabric 1 square to a fabric 2 square (fig 1). Repeat to make four pairs of squares in these fabrics.

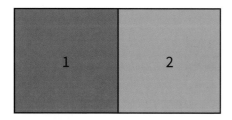

FIG 1

2 Sew a fabric 1 rectangle to the top of the pairs of squares to make unit A (fig 2). Press in the direction indicated by the arrow. Repeat to make four unit A.

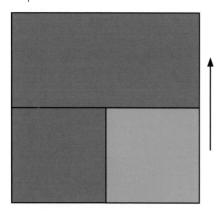

FIG 2

3 Repeat step 1 using fabric 3 and fabric 4 (fig 3).

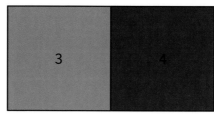

FIG 3

4 Sew a fabric 4 rectangle to the bottom of the pairs of squares to make unit B (fig 4). Press as indicated by the arrow. Repeat to make four unit B.

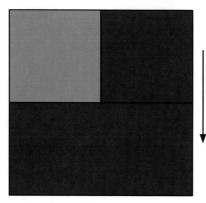

FIG 4

5 Sew a fabric 5 square to a white square (fig 5). Repeat to make eight pairs of squares in these fabrics.

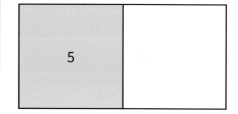

FIG 5

6 Sew a white rectangle to the top of these units to make unit C (fig 6). Press as shown. Repeat to make eight unit C.

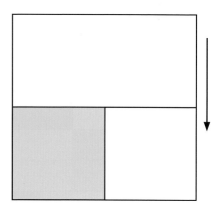

FIG 6

CREATING THE BLOCKS

7 Sew one unit A, one unit B and two unit C together as shown and press in the direction shown by the arrows (fig 7). Repeat to make four blocks.

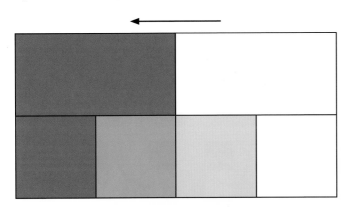

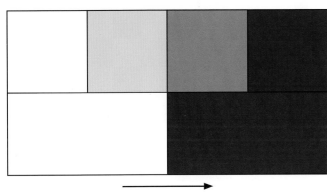

FIG 7

8 Repeat with the other three groups of fabric to make a total of sixteen blocks (fig 8).

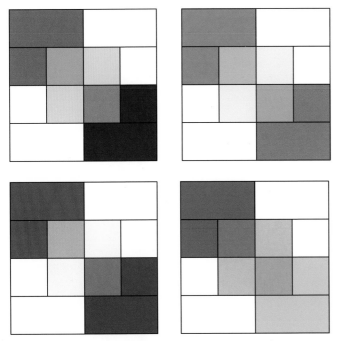

FIG 8

9 Sew the blocks together in four rows of four blocks each, pinning at all seam intersections to ensure a perfect match (fig 9). Press. This should now measure 48½ x 48½in.

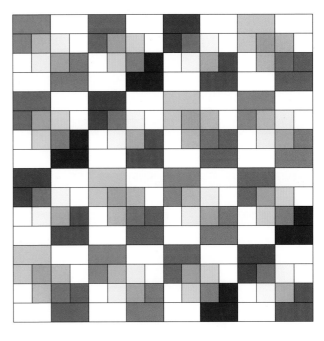

FIG 9

10 Trim two white border strips to measure 2½ x 48½in and sew to the sides of the quilt top. Press. Trim two border strips to measure 2½ x 52½in and sew to the top and bottom of the quilt top (fig 10).

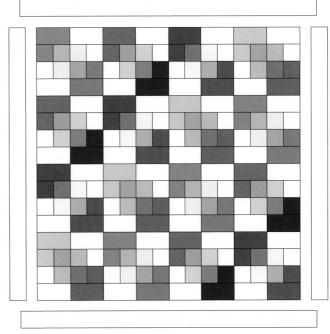

FIG 10

MAKING THE PIECED BORDER

11 From the 2½ x 21in strips from each fabric you have already cut, cut a total of sixteen 2½ x 12in strips and sixteen 2½in squares.

12 Take time playing around with the colours to create the desired effect and when you are happy with the layout, sew four rectangles together with three squares for the side borders and sew four rectangles with five squares for the top and bottom borders as shown (fig 11).

14 Trim two white border strips to measure 2½ x 56½in and sew to the sides of the quilt top. Press. Trim two border strips to measure 2½ x 60½in and sew to the top and bottom of the quilt top (fig 12). Press.

15 Your quilt top is now complete. Quilt as desired and bind to finish (see *General Techniques*).

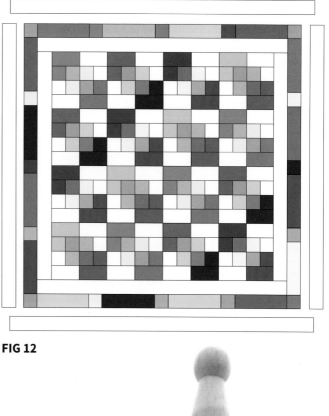

FIG 12

FIG 11

13 Sew the pieced border to the quilt, pinning and easing where necessary.

FABRICS USED

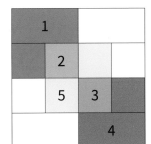

Block 1
1. Tula
2. Taffy
3. Persimmon
4. Snap Dragon
5. Peach Fuzz

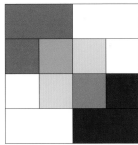

Block 2
1. Stargazer
2. Hibiscus
3. Matcha
4. Tanzanite
5. Mojito

Block 3
1. Iris
2. Cornflower
3. Julep
4. Legendary
5. Whimsy

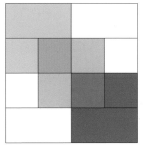

Block 4
1. Pear
2. Cricket
3. Cornflower
4. Carnelian
5. Cerulean

Hidden Butterflies

This is one of those quilts which evolved. It started with playing around with the disappearing nine-patch and trying to create a butterfly block. We changed some of the squares in the nine-patch block to rectangles and had fun discovering what you can do by changing the size of the rectangles. In this block we thought we had created a butterfly block, but having played around with the setting we seem to have lost the butterflies. They are in there somewhere!

This quilt uses fabrics designed by Christopher Wilson-Tate for Moda. It was made by the authors and quilted by The Quilt Room.

Preparation

YOU WILL NEED
- Twenty-three fat quarters, twenty-four if using long quarters
- Scrappy binding made from the excess fabric (see tip on page 48)

SORTING THE FABRICS
- Fabric A, one quarter
- Fabric B, eight quarters
- Fabric C, three quarters
- Fabric D, eight quarters
- Fabric E, three quarters for the sashing strips (four if using long quarters)

The block diagram here (fig 1) shows where the fabrics end up in the finished block.

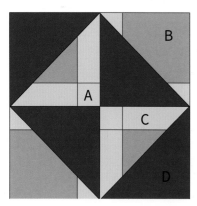

FIG 1

FAT QUARTER CUTTING INSTRUCTIONS
- **Fabric A:** cut one fat quarter into two 4½ x 21in strips and sub-cut eight 4½in squares.
- **Fabric B:** cut each of the eight fat quarters into two 6½in strips and sub-cut each strip into two 6½in squares to make thirty-two. Set the excess aside to make a scrappy binding.
- **Fabric C:** cut each of the three fat quarters into four 4½ x 21in strips and then sub-cut each into three 4½ x 6½in rectangles to make thirty-two (with four spare).
- **Fabric D:** cut each of the eight fat quarters into four 8¼in squares to make thirty-two. From the excess cut a total of nine 2½in squares for the sashing squares.
- **Fabric E:** from each of the three fat quarters cut eight 2½ x 18in strips. It is important to cut the fat quarter this way round. Trim each to measure 2½ x 15¼in rectangles to make a total of twenty-four sashing strips.

LONG QUARTER CUTTING INSTRUCTIONS
- **Fabric A:** cut one long quarter into one 4½ x 42in strip and sub-cut into eight 4½in squares.
- **Fabric B:** cut each of the eight long quarters into one 6½ x 42in strip and sub-cut each strip into four 6½in squares to make thirty-two. Set the excess aside to make a scrappy binding.
- **Fabric C:** cut each of the three long quarters into two 4½ x 42in strips and then sub-cut each into six 4½ x 6½in rectangles to make thirty-two (with four spare).
- **Fabric D:** cut each of the eight long quarters into four 8¼in squares to make thirty-two. From the excess cut a total of nine 2½in squares for the sashing squares.
- **Fabric E:** from each of the four long quarters cut three 2½ x 42in strips and sub-cut each strip into two 2½ x 15¼in strips to make a total of twenty-four sashing strips.

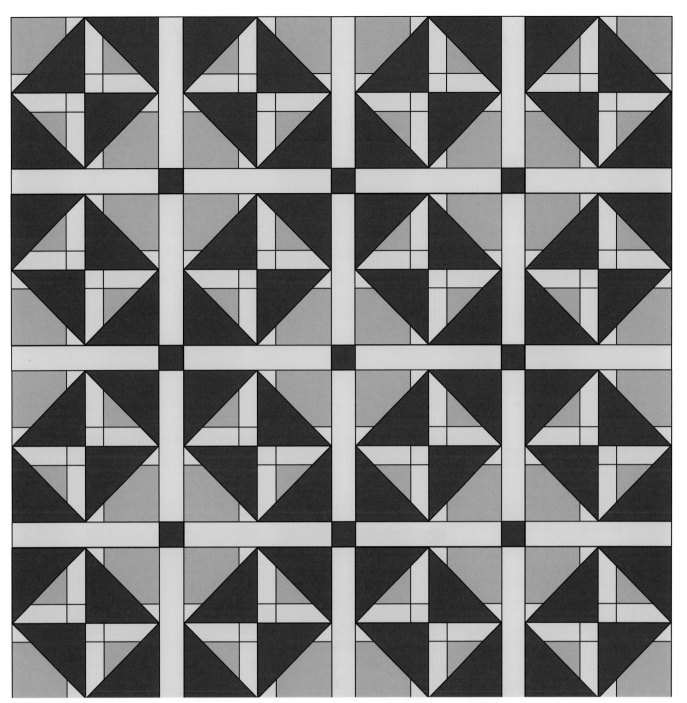

FINISHED SIZE: 65 x 65in (165 x 165cm)

BLOCK SIZE: 14¾in

Making the Quilt

CREATING THE BLOCK UNITS

1 Sew one fabric A 4½in square, four fabric B 6½in squares and four fabric C 4½ x 6½in rectangles together as shown (fig 2). Press. This should measure 16½ x 16½in.

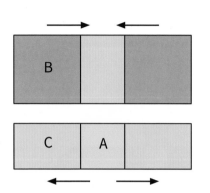
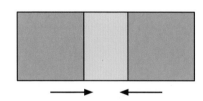
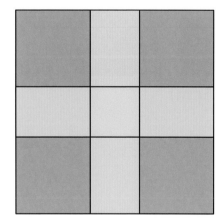

FIG 2

2 Repeat to make eight nine-patch blocks (fig 3).

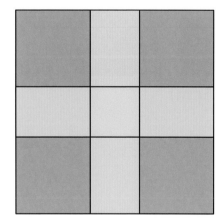

FIG 3

3 Working with one nine-patch block at a time, cut one nine-patch block accurately through the centre in each direction as shown to make four quarters (fig 4).

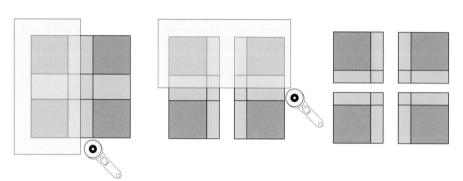

FIG 4

TIP The centre square is 4in wide so the best method of accurately cutting is to line up the 2in mark on your ruler on the seam line.

4 On the **reverse** of one of these quarters, mark the diagonal line from corner to corner, making sure you do not mark through the fabric A square (fig 5).

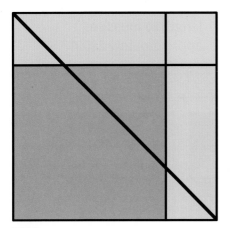

FIG 5

5 Lay this unit right sides together on top of a fabric D 8¼in square aligning the edges. Pin in place. Sew on both sides of the marked diagonal line with a scant ¼in seam allowance (fig 6).

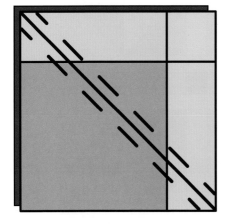

FIG 6

6 Cut along the marked diagonal line and press as shown to reveal two different block units: Block A and Block B (fig 7). Repeat with the other three quarters using the same fabric D.

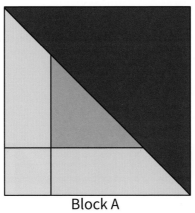

Block A   Block B

FIG 7

7 Sew four units together as shown to make one block (fig 8). Repeat to make two blocks.

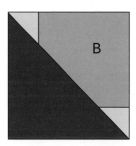

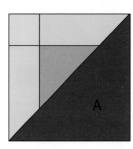

FIG 8

8 Repeat steps 3–7 to make sixteen blocks (fig 9).

FIG 9

9 Lay out the blocks as shown with the sashing strips and the sashing squares. When you are happy with the layout sew the rows together with sashing strips in between. Press as shown (fig 10).

10 Sew the rows together pinning at every seam intersection to ensure a perfect match.

11 Your quilt top is now complete. Quilt as desired and bind to finish (see *General Techniques*).

TIP To make a scrappy binding cut 2½in strips from the excess of fabric B and any other excess strips. Sew into a continuous length to measure approximately 280in.

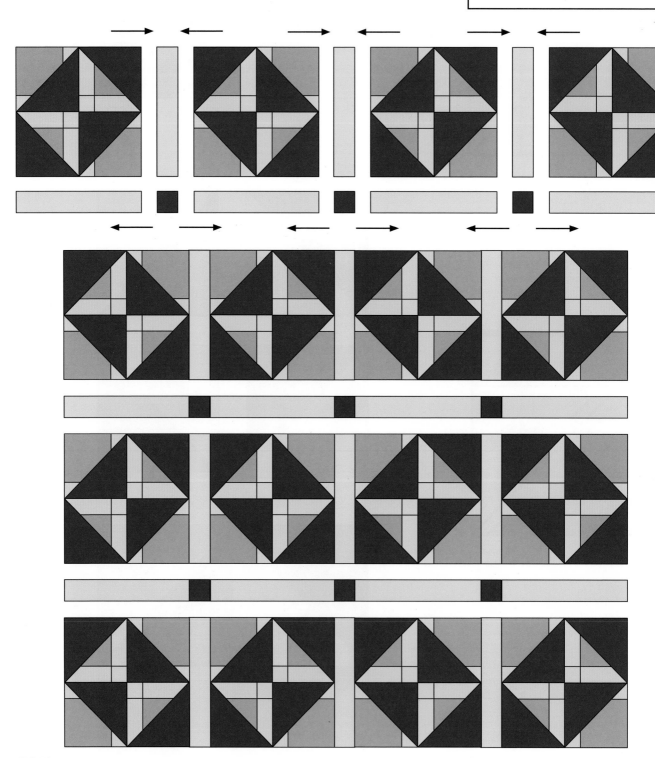

FIG 10

Crazy Hourglass

We used quick piecing techniques to make our hourglass blocks and teamed up seventeen pairs of gorgeous Tula Pink True Colors. We made our quilt ten blocks square but you do have enough fabric to increase the size of the quilt to eleven blocks square if you would like a larger quilt – just cut four 9in squares from each quarter instead of three. See what fun you can have with a simple hourglass block!

This quilt uses True Colors by Tula Pink. It was made by the authors and quilted by The Quilt Room.

Preparation

YOU WILL NEED

- Thirty-four quarters
- ⅝yd (60cm) binding fabric
- Quilting square at least 8in (optional)

SORTING THE FABRICS

Pair up the quarters into seventeen pairs.

FAT AND LONG QUARTER CUTTING INSTRUCTIONS

- Cut each pair of quarters into three pairs of 9in squares

TIP If you carefully press each pair of quarters right sides together you can cut the 9in squares from both fabrics at the same time. You can then mark the diagonals on the top fabric and they will be ready to be sewn.

CUTTING THE OTHER FABRIC
Binding fabric

- Cut eight 2½in strips across the width of the fabric.

FINISHED SIZE: 75½ x 75½in (192 x 192cm)
BLOCK SIZE: 7½in

Making the Quilt

CREATING THE HOURGLASS UNITS

1 Working with one pair of 9in squares, draw diagonal lines from corner to corner in both directions on the wrong side of one of the squares (fig 1).

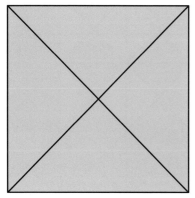

FIG 1

2 With right sides together, lay the marked square on top of the unmarked square. Sew a ¼in seam allowance on both sides of one diagonal line as shown (fig 2). Cut the units apart between stitching, cutting on the drawn line.

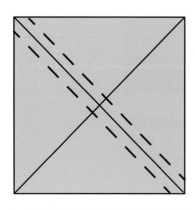

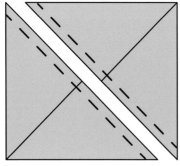

FIG 2

3 Press the units open, pressing seams to the darker fabric (fig 3).

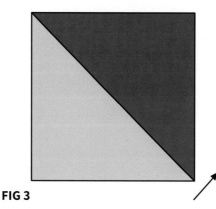

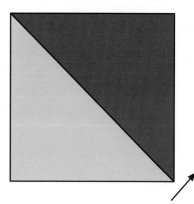

FIG 3

4 On the **reverse** of one unit, continue the drawn line into the other corner. Lay this unit on top of the other unit, right sides together, making sure you have opposite fabrics facing and pin in place. Sew a ¼in seam allowance on both sides of the diagonal line. Cut units apart between the stitching as before (fig 4).

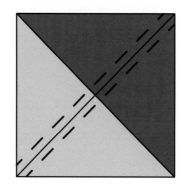

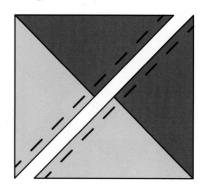

FIG 4

5 Press open to reveal two hourglass blocks (fig 5). Trim to measure 8 x 8in, lining up the diagonal on your quilting square with the diagonal of the blocks. Trim a little from each side so your points still reach into the corner of the square.

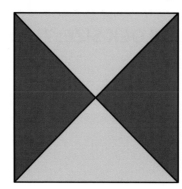

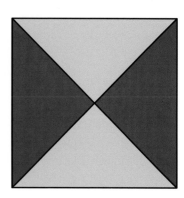

FIG 5

6 Repeat with the other pairs from the same fabric to make six blocks.
7 Repeat with the remaining pairs of fabric to make a total of 102 blocks. You need 100, so two are spare.

ASSEMBLING THE QUILT

8 Lay out the blocks into ten rows of ten blocks (see our suggested layout on page 55). When you are happy with the arrangement, sew the blocks into rows and then sew the rows together, pinning at all seam intersections to ensure a perfect match.

9 Your quilt top is complete. Quilt as desired and bind to finish (see *General Techniques*).

Falling Leaves

Sometimes it is nice to look back at previous quilts for ideas and we certainly had to look *way* back for our inspiration for this one. We found it with Autumn Leaves, a quilt that was featured in Pam's book from 1994! Using the range Windy Days from Tilda, this quilt sprung to mind. We have made a number of changes to the original pattern and absolutely love these gorgeous Tilda fabrics.

This quilt uses Tilda fabrics, and it was made by the authors and quilted by The Quilt Room.

Preparation

YOU WILL NEED
- Seventeen quarters
- ½yd (40cm) fabric for stems
- 4½yd (4.25m) background fabric
- Scrappy binding made from the excess fabric (see tip on page 64)

FAT QUARTER CUTTING INSTRUCTIONS
From each fat quarter cut the following:
- Two 2⅞ x 21in strips and sub-cut each strip into six 2⅞in squares. Cut across the diagonal of each 2⅞in square to make twenty-four small half-square triangles.
- One 4⅞ x 21in strip and sub-cut into three 4⅞in squares. Cut across the diagonal of each 4⅞in square to make six large half-square triangles.

Keep the twenty-four small triangles and the six large triangles from the same fabric together.

Our inspiration for Falling Leaves – a quilt made by Pam in 1994 using a range of Roberta Horton plaids set against a navy background.

LONG QUARTER CUTTING INSTRUCTIONS
- Cut the long quarter into two 9 x 21in rectangles, then follow the instructions for fat quarter cutting.

CUTTING THE OTHER FABRICS
Stem fabric
- Cut twelve 1 x 42in strips.

Background fabric
- Cut twenty-nine 2⅞ x 42in strips and sub-cut each strip into fourteen 2⅞in squares to make a total of 400 squares (you will have six spare). Cut each square in half diagonally to make 800 half-square triangles.

- Refold the remainder of the fabric (approx 72in) *lengthways* and cut the following down the length of the fabric: four 2in wide strips for the borders (these can be trimmed to size later), nine 1¼in wide strips for the horizontal sashing strips (these can be trimmed to size later), two 6½in wide strips and sub-cut into ninety 1¼ x 6½in vertical sashing strips, four 2½in wide strips and sub-cut each strip into twenty-five 2½in squares to make a total of one hundred 2½in squares.

FINISHED SIZE: 69¾ x 69¾in (177 x 177cm)

BLOCK SIZE: 6in

Falling Leaves 61

Making the Quilt

CREATING THE STEM UNIT

1 To make the stems, sew 100 background fabric triangles to one side of the 1in wide strips allocated for the stems, leaving approximately 1in between the triangles to allow for squaring up the squares (see step 3). You will get approximately nine per strip (fig 1). Finger press the triangles open.

2 Sew another one hundred background triangles to the other side of the strip, matching the tips of the triangles as shown (fig 2). Press the triangles open (fig 3) and then cut the strip between them.

3 Use a quilting square to trim the unit to measure 2½in square. It is important to place the diagonal line of the quilting square on the centre of the stem when trimming the unit (fig 4).

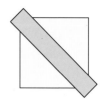

FIG 4

4 Sew two background fabric triangles to the stem unit as shown, making sure your stem is facing the correct way (fig 5). Press and trim the dog ears to create a straight edge.

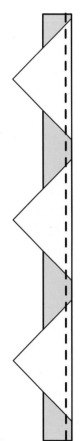

FIG 1

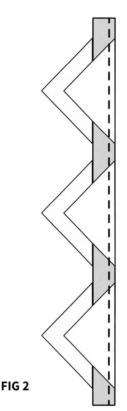

FIG 2

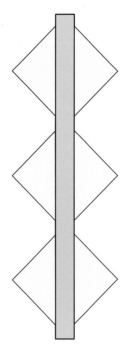

FIG 3

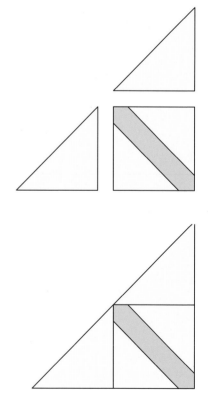

FIG 5

PIECING THE BLOCKS

5 Working with one fabric at a time, take a large triangle and sew to the stem unit as shown (fig 6). Press. Repeat to make six of these units.

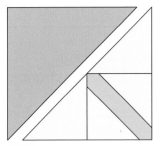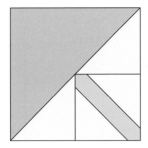

FIG 6

6 Take twenty-four small triangles and twenty-four background triangles and sew together to make twenty-four half-square units (fig 7). Press.

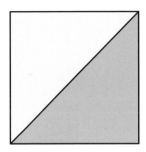

FIG 7

7 Sew two half-square units together with a backgound square as shown (fig 8).

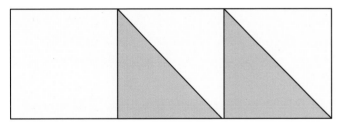

FIG 8

8 Sew two half-square units together as shown (fig 9). Press. Repeat to make six.

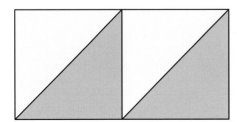

FIG 9

9 Referring to the block diagram, sew the units together as shown (fig 10). Be sure to use matching fabrics in each leaf block. Press. At this stage we found it useful to press some seams open.

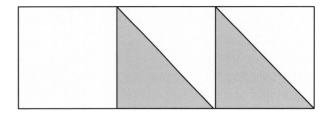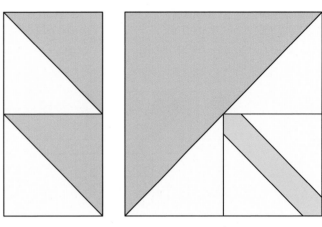

FIG 10

10 Repeat with the remaining fabrics to make one hundred leaf blocks (fig 11).

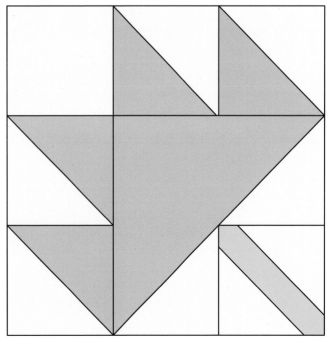

FIG 11

ASSEMBLING THE QUILT

11 Assemble the blocks in ten horizontal rows of ten blocks each, adding 1¼ x 6½in vertical sashing strips between the blocks. Rotate the leaf blocks as shown to form the pattern (fig 12).

12 Measure the width of your rows and trim the nine horizontal sashing strips to this measurement. They will be approximately 70in long.

13 Sew the rows together with the nine sashing strips in between, pinning and easing where necessary and making sure the vertical sashing strips are aligned.

14 Determine the vertical measurement from top to bottom through the centre of your quilt top. Trim two side borders to this measurement. Pin and sew to the quilt. Determine the horizontal measurement from side to side across the centre of the quilt top. Trim two borders to this measurement.

Sew to the top and bottom of your quilt and press.

15 Your quilt top is complete. Quilt as desired and bind to finish (see *General Techniques*).

TIP To make a scrappy border cut 2½in strips from excess quarters and join into a continuous length of approximately 300in.

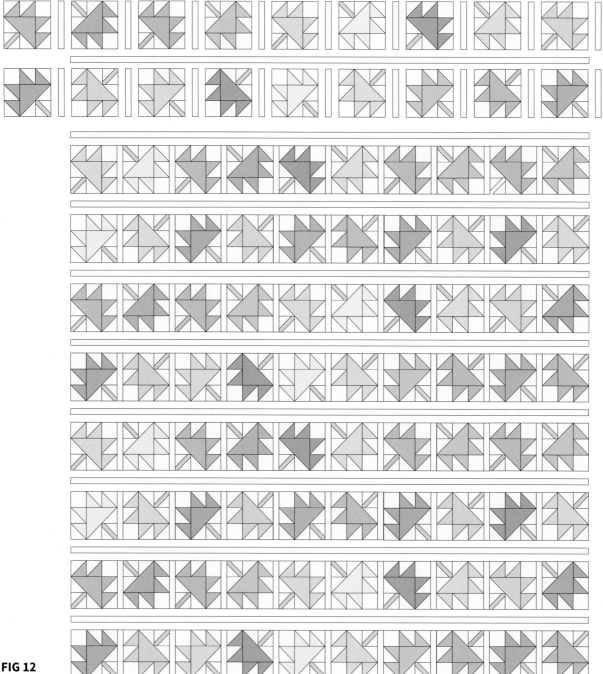

FIG 12

Diamond Sparkle

We loved the three dimensional effect this quilt created when using four shades of grey (sounds like a book!) to frame the diamonds. Our pattern gives instructions for just four fabrics to frame the diamonds but we couldn't resist using a range of fabrics in each shade for a scrappier effect.

This quilt uses fabrics designed by Alison Glass for Andover Fabrics. It was made by the authors and quilted by The Quilt Room.

Preparation

YOU WILL NEED

- Fifteen quarters for the diamonds
- ¾yd (70cm) each of four shades of grey for sashing – can range from white to black
- ⅝yd (60cm) border fabric
- ⅝yd (60cm) binding fabric
- 60° triangle tool measuring at least 8½in

FAT QUARTER CUTTING INSTRUCTIONS

- Cut each of the fifteen fat quarters into two 8½ x 21in strips. You will have thirty 8½ x 21in strips.

LONG QUARTER CUTTING INSTRUCTIONS

- Cut each of the fifteen long quarters into one 8½ x 42in strip. You will have fifteen 8½ x 42in strips.

CUTTING THE OTHER FABRICS

Sashing fabric
- Cut each of the four sashing fabrics into three 8½ x 42in strips. You will have twelve 8½ x 42in strips.

Border fabric
- Cut eight 2½in strips across the width of the fabric.

Binding fabric
- Cut eight 2½in wide across the width of the fabric.

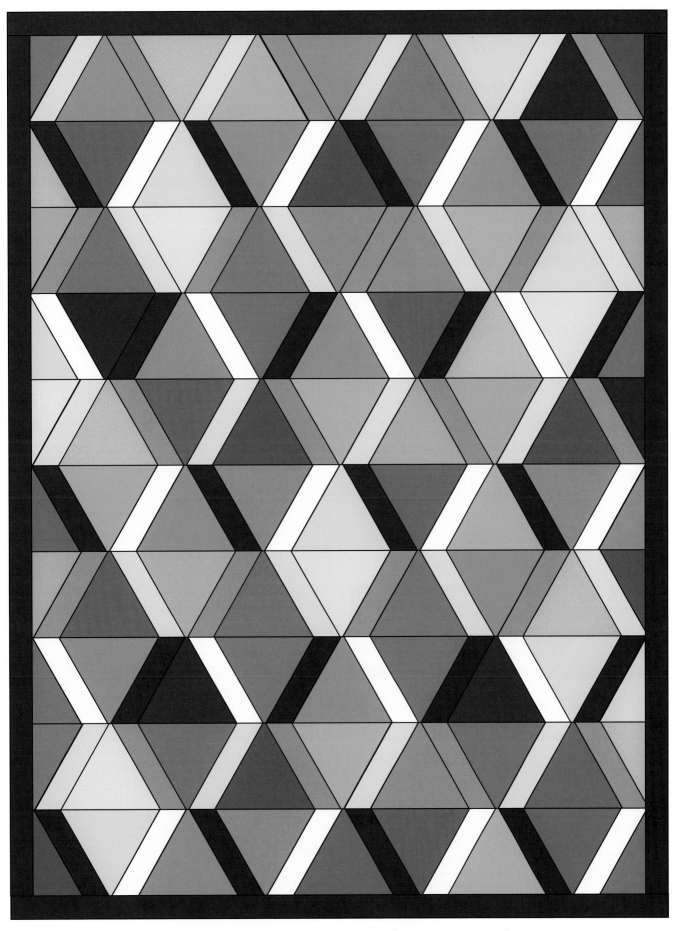

FINISHED SIZE: 70 x 84in (178 x 213cm)

Diamond Sparkle 69

Making the Quilt

CUTTING THE TRIANGLES AND SASHING

1 Place one 8½in wide strip allocated for the diamonds on the cutting mat. *This will be 21in long when using fat quarters and 42in long when using long quarters. You can keep the 42in long strip folded to cut two triangles at a time.* Place the 60° triangle tool on the left side of the strip unit as shown aligning the 8½in line of the triangle with the bottom of the strip and the cut off top of the triangle with the top of the strip (fig 1). Cut your first triangle.

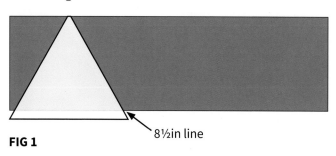

8½in line

FIG 1

2 Rotate the triangle tool 180° and cut the second triangle (fig 2). Next rotate back 180° and cut a third triangle. You now have three triangles from the 8½ x 21in strip and six triangles from the 8½ x 42in strip.

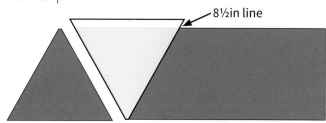

8½in line

FIG 2

3 Repeat with all the 8½in wide strips allocated for the diamonds to make a total of ninety triangles.

> **TIP** You can layer strips on top of each other so you can cut more than one strip at a time.

4 Take one grey sashing strip and lay it on the cutting mat, keeping it folded. This allows you to cut a right and a left sashing strip at the same time. Lay a quilting ruler on the right hand side of the strip lining up the 60° marker of the ruler along the bottom of the strip and cut the strip at a 60° angle (fig 3). *You can also use a 60° triangle tool to do this.*

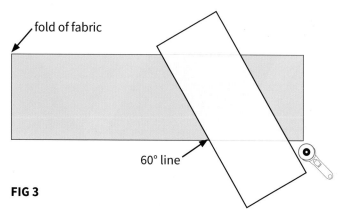

fold of fabric

60° line

FIG 3

5 Rotate the strip 180° and using your quilting ruler line up the 3½in line along the edge of the strip (fig 4). Cut the first sashing piece. Continue along the strips to cut four pairs of sashing strips making sure you are always cutting at a 60° angle and always aligning the 3½in line on your ruler. You will have four strips angled one way and four angled the other.

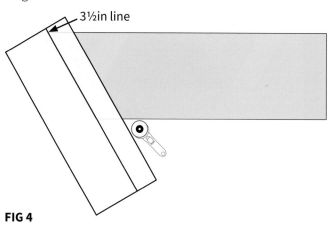

3½in line

FIG 4

6 Repeat with all twelve sashing strips to make a total of twelve pairs of sashing strips in each of the four shades of grey (fig 5).

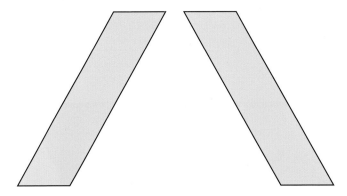

FIG 5

ASSEMBLING THE QUILT

7 At this stage you need to lay out all the triangles as per fig 6 to be sure you sew the right shade sashing strip to each triangle. There are ten rows of nine triangles each. To create a 3D effect you need to have different shades of sashing strip around each diamond. In rows one, three, five, seven and nine alternate the two middle shades of grey across the rows. In rows two, four, six, eight and ten alternate the darkest and the lightest across the rows.

FIG 6

8 When you are happy with the layout, sew the triangles and sashing strips together to form rows. You will notice that when sewing the sashing strips to the triangles there is a ¼in overlap at each end. This is because you have an angled cut. Press to the sashing strips so your triangles lay flat (fig 7).

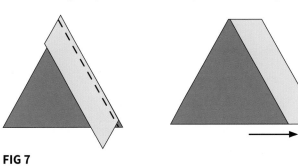

FIG 7

9 Continue adding triangles and sashing strips, rotating alternate triangles 180°. Sew together nine triangles and eight sashing strips as shown (fig 8).

FIG 8

10 Repeat to make ten rows and sew the rows together, pinning at all seam intersections to ensure a perfect match (fig 9). As you have always pressed towards the sashing strips your seams will not nest together but as they are angled it is fine.

FIG 9

Diamond Sparkle 71

ADDING THE BORDERS

11 Join your 2½in border strips into one continuous length. Determine the vertical measurement from top to bottom through the centre of your quilt top. Join and cut two side borders to this measurement. Pin and sew to the quilt to form a straight edge (fig 10). Press and trim the excess fabric.

12 Determine the horizontal measurement from side to side across the centre of the quilt top. Cut two borders to this measurement. Sew to the top and bottom of your quilt and press.

13 Your quilt top is now complete. Quilt and bind as desired (see *General Techniques*).

FIG 10

Diamond Sparkle 73

Octagon Stars

Partial seaming can help create some gorgeous effects that give a swirling sense of movement to a design. In this quilt we have used this technique to create our octagon stars. Note that there's a template for the octagon at the end of the book, but we've also given instructions on how to draft your own.

This quilt uses The Seamstress by Edyta Sitar for Andover Fabrics. It was made by the authors and quilted by The Quilt Room.

Preparation

YOU WILL NEED

- Twenty quarters
- 3½ yd (3¼m) background fabric
- ⅝yd (60cm) binding fabric, or a scrappy binding can be made from the excess fabric (see tip on page 82 for instructions)

SORTING THE FABRICS

- Choose four quarters for the octagon centres of the stars.
- The remaining sixteen quarters will make the octagon surrounds and the sashing squares. Pair up the quarters so you have eight pairs for the octagon surrounds. Each pair will make two blocks or you can mix and match to make sixteen different blocks as we have done.

FAT QUARTER CUTTING INSTRUCTIONS

- From the four fat quarters allocated for the octagon centres cut two 7 x 21in strips from each quarter and cut two octagons from each strip using the template on page 112 (or see tip opposite) to make a total of sixteen octagons.
- From each of the sixteen fat quarters allocated for the octagon surrounds cut two 5⅜ x 21in strips and sub-cut into four 5⅜in squares. Cut across the diagonal of each of the four squares to make a total of eight triangles from each fat quarter.
- Also from the sixteen fat quarters allocated for the octagon surrounds cut one 2½in square for the sashing squares. You only need nine but you can choose which nine later.

LONG QUARTER CUTTING INSTRUCTIONS

- From the four long quarters allocated for the octagon centres cut one 7 x 42in from each long quarter and cut four octagons from each strip using the template on page 112 (or see tip opposite) to make a total of sixteen octagons.
- From each of the sixteen long quarters allocated for the octagon surrounds cut one 5⅜ x 42in strip and sub-cut into four 5⅜in squares. Cut across the diagonal of each square to make a total of eight triangles from each long quarter.
- Also from the sixteen long quarters allocated for the octagon surrounds cut one 2½in square for the sashing squares. You only need nine in total but you can choose which nine later.

CUTTING THE OTHER FABRICS
Background fabric
■ Cut eight 5 x 42in strips and sub-cut each strip into eight 5in squares to make a total of sixty-four squares.
■ Cut five 5⅜ x 42in strips and sub-cut each strip into seven 5⅜in squares. Cut across the diagonal of each square to make a total of seventy triangles. You only need sixty-four so six will be spare.
■ Cut nineteen 2½ x 42in strips. Sub-cut twelve of these into twenty-four 2½ x 15¾in rectangles and set the remaining seven background fabric strips aside for the borders.

Binding fabric
■ Cut eight 2½in wide strips across the width of the fabric.

TIP You can use the octagon template supplied (see page 112) or if you would like to draw your own here are the instructions:
Draw a line which measures 2⅞in using your quilting ruler. Line up the 45° marker on your quilting ruler on this line and draw the next side of the octagon at an angle of 45°. Measure that line at 2⅞in and continue drawing each side at 45°. Once you have drawn the octagon double check that each side measures 2⅞in before using it as a template to cut out the octagons from fabric.

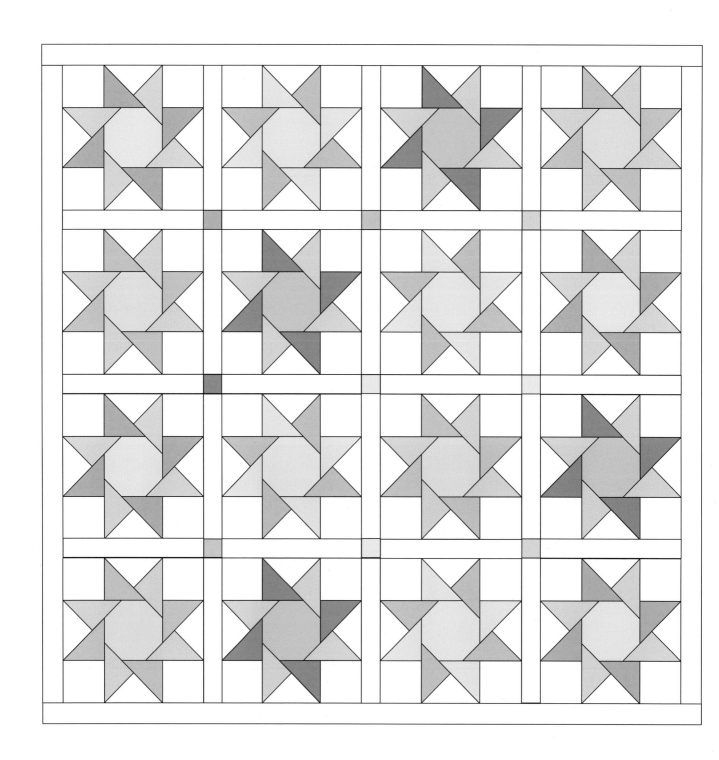

FINISHED SIZE: 71in x 71in (180 x 180cm)
BLOCK SIZE: 15¼in

Making the Quilt

MAKING THE OCTAGON STAR BLOCKS

1 Working with one pair of fabrics at a time, allocate one of the pair to be fabric A and one to be fabric B. With right sides together, making sure that the bottom of the triangle aligns with the bottom of the square, sew one fabric A triangle to a 5in background square to make unit A (fig 1). Note that the triangle will overlap at the top by ¼in. Repeat to make four unit A. Press.

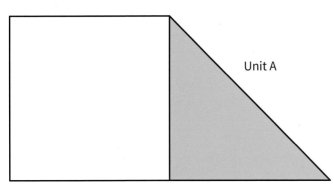

FIG 1

2 With right sides together, sew one fabric B triangle to a background triangle to make unit B (fig 2). Repeat to make four unit B. Press.

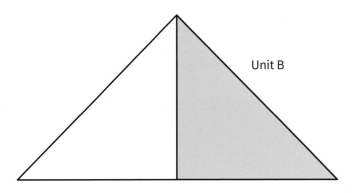

FIG 2

3 Take one unit A and, with right sides together, sew it to one side of the octagon. Sew only half of the seam as shown. Note that the corner of your triangle will overlap the octagon as shown (fig 3).

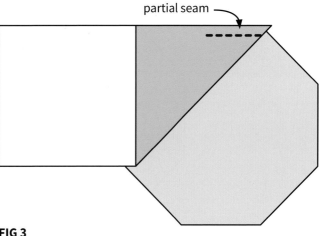

FIG 3

4 Gently press. The triangle you have sewn and the next octagon side will now have a straight edge (fig 4). Remember you are still dealing with bias edges so handle carefully and do not use steam.

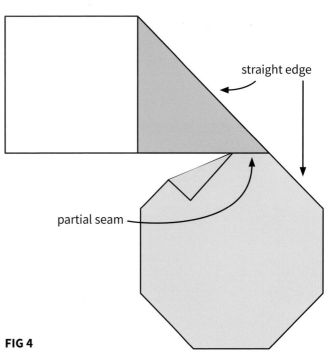

FIG 4

5 Take a unit B and, with right sides together, sew it to the first triangle as shown (fig 5). Press open.

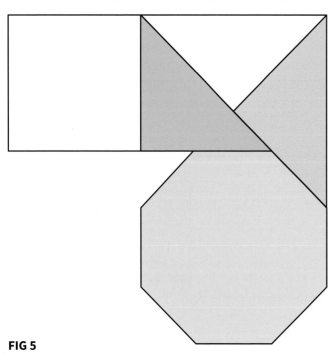

FIG 5

6 Take a unit A and, with right sides together, sew it to the second triangle as shown (fig 6). Press open.

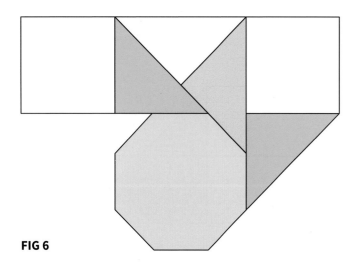

FIG 6

7 Take a unit B and sew it to the third triangle as shown (fig 7). Press open.

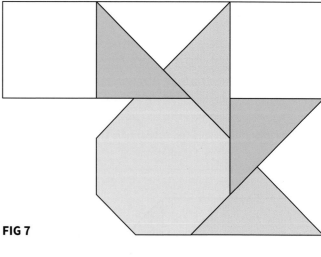

FIG 7

8 Take a unit A and sew it to the fourth triangle as shown (fig 8). Press open.

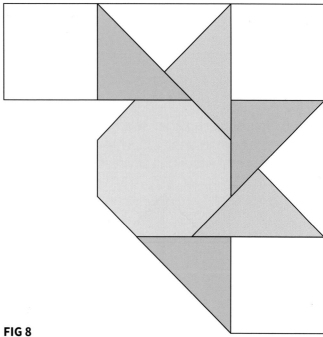

FIG 8

9 Continue sewing alternating units A and B until you have sewn the last unit. You can then complete the first partial seam (fig 9). Press. Your block will measure approximately 15¾in square. Square the block to exactly 15¾in square making sure you don't cut off any star points.

10 Repeat with all pairs of quarters to make sixteen octagon stars. You can either make two of each block or mix and match units A and B so you have sixteen different blocks.

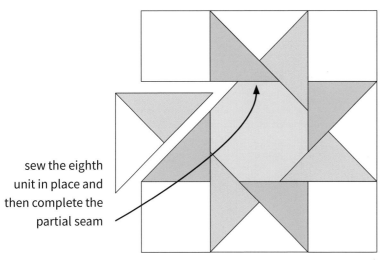

sew the eighth unit in place and then complete the partial seam

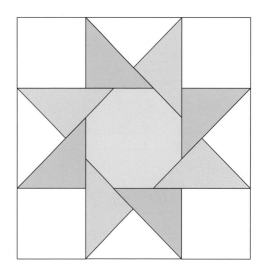

FIG 9

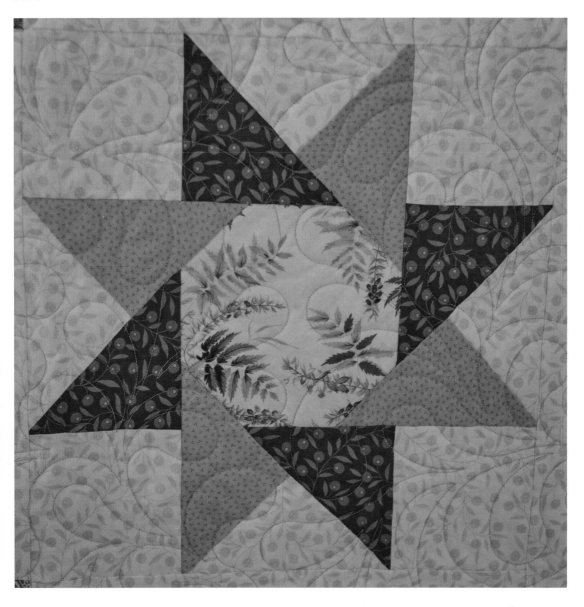

ASSEMBLING THE QUILT

11 Lay out the blocks in four rows of four blocks each and place the sashing strips in between the blocks with a sashing square in place (fig 10).

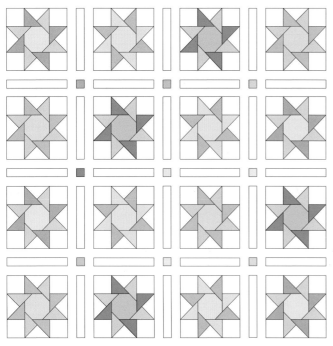

FIG 10

12 When you are happy with the layout, sew the blocks into rows and then sew the rows together with the sashing strips in between. Always press towards the sashing strips and the seams will nest together nicely (fig 11).

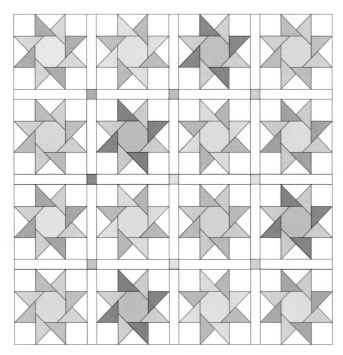

FIG 11

13 Join your 2½in border strips into one continuous length. Determine the vertical measurement from top to bottom through the centre of your quilt top. Cut two side borders to this measurement. Pin and sew to the quilt. Determine the width across the centre of the quilt top. Cut two borders to this measurement. Sew to the top and bottom and press (fig 12).

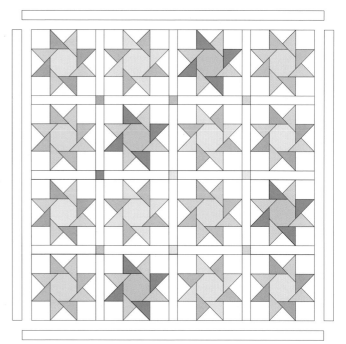

FIG 12

14 Your quilt is complete. Quilt as desired and bind to finish (see *General Techniques*).

> **TIP** To make a scrappy binding, cut 2½in strips from the excess fabric and sew into a continuous length of approximately 300in.

Spotlight

This is the perfect quilt to showcase a feature fabric in the centre. We used an Alice in Wonderland image from Tula Pink's Curiouser & Curiouser range, but by choosing any special fabric for your 'spotlight' – or even printing a photo onto fabric – this will become a unique and extra special quilt.

This quilt uses the range Curiouser & Curiouser by Tula Pink. We wanted to show how highlighting one fabric in the spotlight can create a quilt that will be extra special to someone. It was made by the authors and quilted by The Quilt Room.

Preparation

YOU WILL NEED
- Thirteen quarters
- 2yd (1.7m) background fabric
- Scrappy binding made from the excess fabric (see tip on page 94)
- 90⁰ triangle tool measuring at least 6½in high (optional), or a 10in quilting square or larger can be used

SORTING THE FABRICS
- Choose one quarter for the centre of the quilt.
- Choose eight quarters for the triangles around the octagon.
- Choose one quarter for the 3in friendship star blocks.
- The remaining three quarters are for the 9in friendship star blocks and outer border.

> **TIP** Some fabrics deserve to be fussy cut and it is worth the extra time to do it.

FAT QUARTER CUTTING INSTRUCTIONS

From the quarter allocated for the centre of the quilt
- Cut one 9 x 21in strip and then use the template on page 113 (follow the instructions to make the complete shape) or make your own template (see tip on page 88), to cut one octagon.
- Cut one 3⅞ x 21in strip and sub-cut into two 3⅞in squares and one 3½in square. Cut across the diagonal of both 3⅞in squares to make four triangles. *When the fabric is directional if you cut the two squares in different directions the fabric will be the right way round when sewn.* Do not cut the 3½in square.

From each of the eight quarters allocated for the octagon surround
- Cut one 6½ x 21in strip and set aside to cut a large 90⁰ triangle. *For directional fabric you may need to change the way you cut to ensure the pattern is facing the way you want it.*
- Cut one 3⅞ x 21in strip then sub-cut into two 3⅞in squares and one 3½in square. Cut across the diagonal of both 3⅞in squares to make four triangles. *When the fabric is directional if you cut the squares in a different direction the fabric will be the right way round when sewn.* Do not cut the 3½in square.

From each of the three additional quarters for the 9in friendship star blocks
- Cut one 3⅞ x 21in strip and sub-cut into two 3⅞in squares and one 3½in square. Cut across the diagonal of both 3⅞in squares to make four triangles. Do not cut the 3½in square.
- From two of the quarters cut five 2½ x 21in strips for the outer border.

From the quarter allocated for the 3in friendship star blocks
- Cut one 1½ x 21in strip and sub-cut into twelve 1½in squares.
- Cut three 1⅞ x 21in strips and sub-cut into twenty-four 1⅞in squares.
- Cut across the diagonal of each 1⅞in square to make forty-eight small triangles.

LONG QUARTER CUTTING INSTRUCTIONS
From the quarter allocated for the centre of the quilt
- Cut one octagon using the template on page 113 as close to one end of the long quarter as possible.
- From the remainder of the long quarter, trim to measure 3⅞in wide and sub-cut into two 3⅞in squares and one 3½in square. Cut across the diagonal of both 3⅞in squares to make four triangles. Do not cut the 3½in square. *When the fabric is directional if you cut the two squares in different directions the fabric will be the right way round when sewn.*

From each of the eight quarters allocated for the octagon surround
- Cut in half to make two rectangles 9 x 21in.
- From one rectangle cut one 6½ x 21in strip and set aside to cut a large 90⁰ triangle.
- From the second rectangle cut one 3⅞ x 21in strip and sub-cut into two 3⅞in squares and one 3½in square. Cut across the diagonal of both 3⅞in squares to make four triangles. Do not cut the 3½in square. *When the fabric is directional if you cut the squares in a different direction the fabric will be the right way round when sewn.*

From each of the two additional quarters used for the 9in friendship star blocks
- Cut two 2½ x 42in strips for the outer borders.
- Cut one 3⅞ x 42in strip and sub-cut into two 3⅞in squares and one 3½in square.
- Cut across the diagonal of both 3⅞in squares to make four triangles. Do not cut the 3½in square.
- Trim the balance of the strip to measure 2½in wide and cut a strip approximately 2½ x 30in to add to the outer border strips.

From the third additional quarter used for the 9in friendship star blocks
- Cut one 3⅞ x 42in strip and sub-cut into two 3⅞in squares and one 3½in square.
- Cut across the diagonal of both 3⅞in squares to make four triangles. Do not cut the 3½in square.

From the quarter allocated for the 3in friendship star blocks
- Cut one 1½ x 42in strip and sub-cut into twelve 1½in squares.
- Cut two 1⅞ x 42in strips and sub-cut into twenty-four 1⅞in squares.
- Cut across the diagonal of each 1⅞in square to make forty-eight small triangles.

CUTTING THE BACKGROUND FABRIC
- Cut one 7 x 42in strip then sub-cut two 7in squares. Cut across the diagonal of each square to make four corner triangles for the central block.
- Cut two 1½ x 42in strips then sub-cut into forty-eight 1½in squares.
- Cut two 1⅞ x 42in strips then sub-cut into twenty-four 1⅞in squares. Cut across the diagonal of all the 1⅞in squares to make forty-eight triangles for the 3in friendship star blocks.

Re-fold the fabric *lengthways* (it will be approx 52in) and cut the following:
- Four 2½ x 52in strips for the middle border (to be trimmed later).
- One 3½ x 52in strip then sub-cut into eight 3½ x 6½in rectangles.
- Four 3½ x 52in strips then sub-cut into fifty-six 3½in squares
- Two 3¾ x 52in strips then sub-cut each strip into one 3¾ x 21in and one 3¾ x 27½in rectangle to make two of each for the inner border.
- Two 3⅞ x 52in strips then sub-cut into twenty-four 3⅞in squares. Cut across the diagonal of all the 3⅞in squares to make forty-eight triangles for the 9in friendship star blocks.

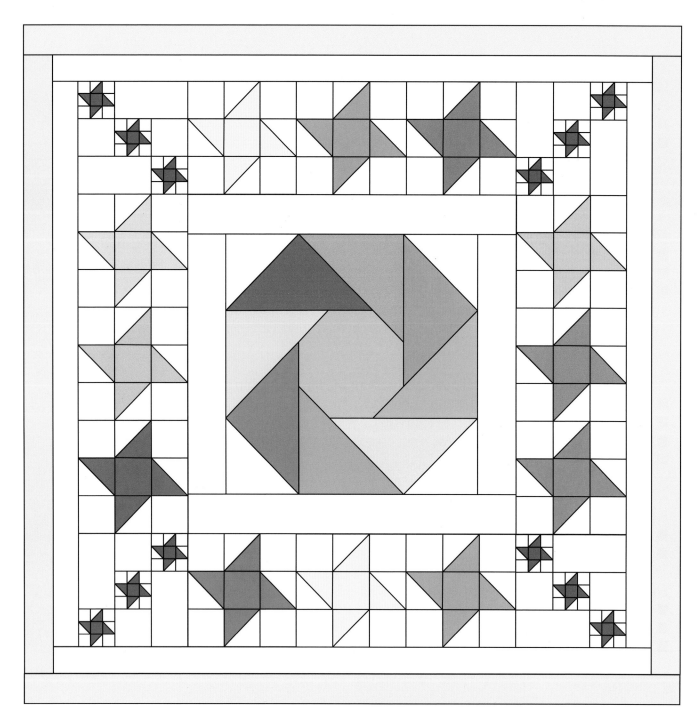

FINISHED SIZE: 53 x 53in (135 x 135cm)

TIP You can use the octagon template supplied (see page 113) or if you would like to draw your own here are the instructions:

Draw a line which measures 3¾in using your quilting ruler. Line up the 45° marker on your quilting ruler on this line and draw the next side of the octagon at an angle of 45°. Measure that line at 3¾in and continue drawing each side at 45°. Once you have drawn the octagon double check that each side measures 3¾in before using it as a template to cut out the octagons from fabric.

Making the Quilt

CREATING THE CENTRAL BLOCK

1 Place the 90° triangle tool on one of the 6½ x 21in rectangles, lining up the 6½in line along the bottom of the strip unit and the cut off top of the ruler along the top (fig 1). Cut one triangle. If you are using a quilting square, position it with the 0 at the top and place some tape from 9⅜in on the left to 9⅜in on the right. This is your guide to place along the bottom edge. Repeat with all eight rectangles allocated for the central block.

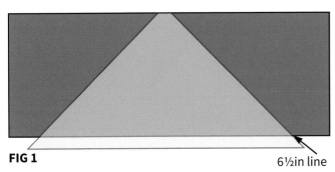

FIG 1   6½in line

2 Take one triangle for the central octagon surround and, with right sides together, sew it to one side of the octagon. Sew only *half* of the seam as shown. Note that the corner of your triangle will overlap the octagon as shown (fig 2).

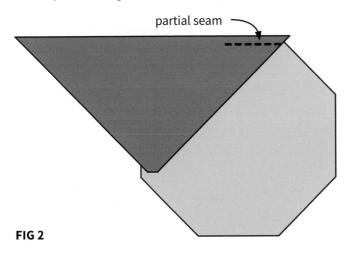

partial seam

FIG 2

3 Gently press. The triangle you have sewn and the next octagon side will now have a straight edge (fig 3). Remember you are still dealing with bias edges so handle carefully and do not use steam.

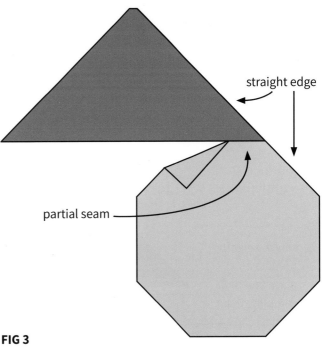

straight edge

partial seam

FIG 3

4 Take another triangle and, with right sides together, sew it to the first triangle as shown. Press open (fig 4).

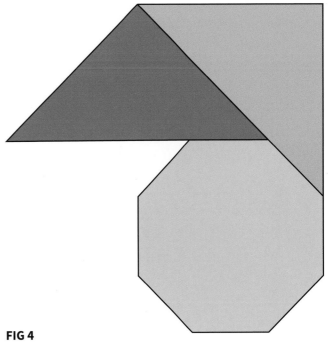

FIG 4

5 Take another triangle and, with right sides together, sew it to the second triangle as shown. Press open (fig 5).

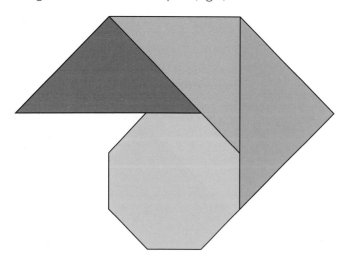

FIG 5

6 Continue sewing the triangles to the octagon. When you have sewn the eighth triangle you can complete the first partial seam (fig 6).

sew the eighth triangle in place and then complete the partial seam

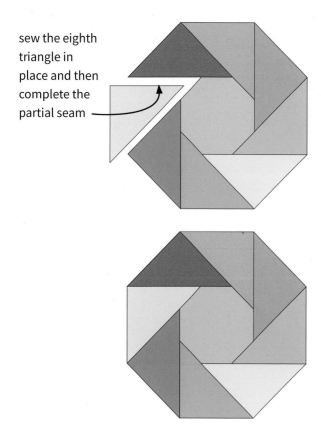

FIG 6

7 Sew a corner triangle to each corner to complete the block, and then press (fig 7). Trim the corners to square up the block if necessary. Your block should measure 21in square.

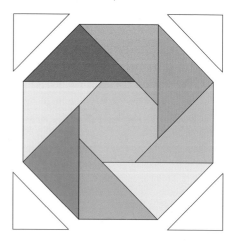

FIG 7

8 Sew the 3¾ x 21in background strips to the sides of the block and the 3¾ x 27½in strips to the top and bottom (fig 8). Press.

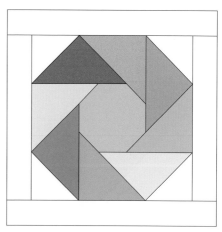

FIG 8

MAKING THE 9in FRIENDSHIP STARS

9 Working with one fabric at a time, sew four triangles and four background triangles together to make four half-square triangle units. Press as shown (fig 9).

10 Sew the half-square triangle units together as shown with four 3½in background squares. Press as shown (fig 10).

11 Repeat to make twelve blocks in total, using each of the twelve fabrics (fig 11).

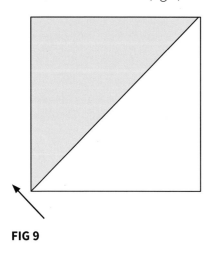

FIG 9

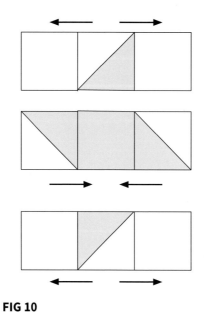

FIG 10

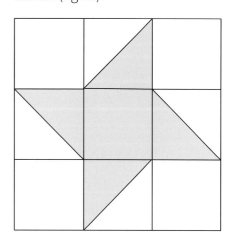

FIG 11

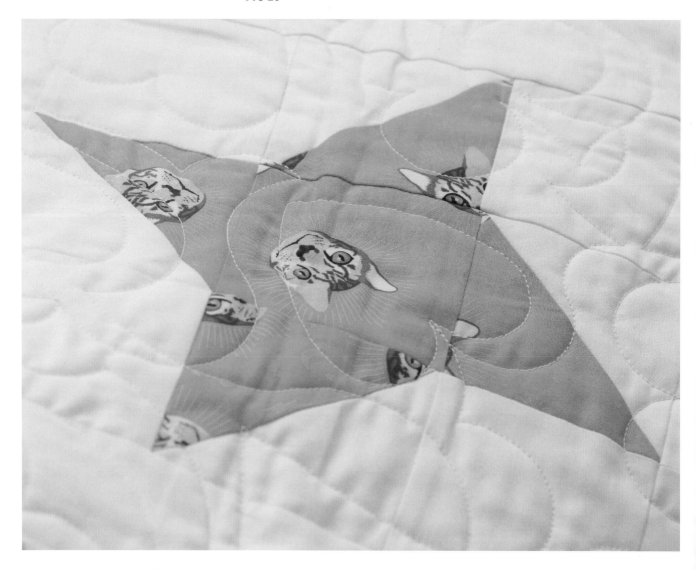

MAKING THE SMALL FRIENDSHIP STARS

12 Using the triangles allocated for the 3in friendship stars and small background triangles, sew together to make forty-eight half-square triangle units (fig 12).

FIG 12

13 Sew four half-square triangle units, one 1½in square and four 1½in background squares together to make one 3in block (finished size) (fig 13). Make twelve blocks.

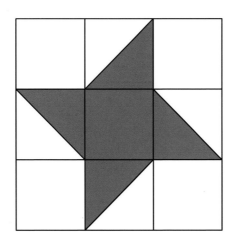

FIG 13

14 Sew three 3in star blocks together with two 3½ x 6½in background rectangles and two 3½in background squares (fig 14).

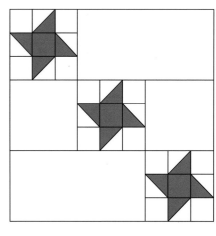

FIG 14

ASSEMBLING THE QUILT

15 Lay out the blocks as shown and when you are happy with the layout, sew all the units together as shown (fig 15). Press.

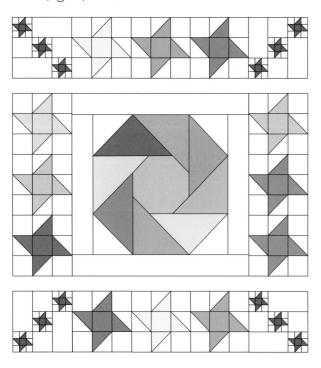

FIG 15

16 Determine the vertical measurement from top to bottom through the centre of your quilt top. Trim two side borders to this size. Pin and sew to the quilt. Next determine the horizontal measurement from side to side across the centre of the quilt top. Trim two borders to this measurement. Sew to the top and bottom of your quilt and press (fig 16).

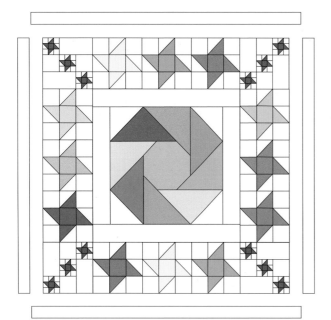

FIG 16

17 Your outer border can be as fun as you like. We sewed the 2½in wide strips of one fabric allocated for the outer borders together and added one fabric to two sides and the other fabric to the other two sides. You could fussy cut some teacups to each corner or add little extra squares. You do have spare fabric to play with. Sew the borders as in step 16 (fig 17).

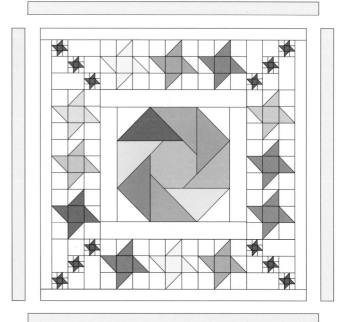

FIG 17

18 Your quilt is complete. Quilt as desired and bind to finish (see *General Techniques*).

TIP To make a scrappy binding, cut 2½in strips from your excess fabric and join together to create a length of approx. 230in.

Spotlight 95

Fun of the Fair

This quilt is not a difficult one to piece as it is comprised of just two units – a square within a square and a triangle within a square. The placement of the fabrics is the time-consuming part and you do need some space to lay out the units before sewing. There are many various ways of placing the fabrics and the quilt will become totally unique to you. Look out for our bonus quilt too!

This quilt uses thirties reproduction prints from the Dutch Heritage 1930s range. It was made by the authors and quilted by The Quilt Room.

Preparation

YOU WILL NEED
- Thirty quarters
- ½yd (0.5m) binding fabric
- Creative Grids 'Two Peaks in One' ruler, or use the templates on page 113

FAT QUARTER CUTTING INSTRUCTIONS
- Choose eight fat quarters and cut four 8½in squares from each to make thirty-two 8½in squares.
- From the twenty-two remaining fat quarters cut four 4½ x 21in strips from each to make a total of eighty-eight 4½ x 21in strips.

LONG QUARTER CUTTING INSTRUCTIONS
- Choose eight long quarters and cut four 8½in squares from each to make thirty-two 8½in squares.
- From the twenty-two remaining long quarters cut two 4½ x 42in strips from each and cut in half to make a total of eighty-eight 4½ x 21in strips.

PREPARING THE FABRICS FOR ONE BLOCK

It is preferable to work one block at a time. Once the units for each block are made and partially sewn together, they need to be set aside until all blocks are ready to sew. The quilt is sewn together row by row so it is not until everything is decided upon that sewing the rows can begin. The diagram shows the pieces in different colours for identification (fig 1).

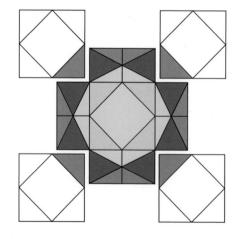

FIG 1

For one block you need:
- One 8½in square for centre snowball unit (yellow).
- One 4½ x 21in strip cut into four 4½in squares for corners of centre snowball unit (lilac).
- One 4½ x 21in strip for inner side triangles in triangle in square unit (green).
- Two 4½ x 21in strips of the same fabric for centre triangle in triangle in square unit (navy).
- Two 4½in x 21in strips of the same fabric – one for the outer side triangles in triangle in square unit (pink), the other cut into four 4½in squares for corners of outer snowball blocks (pink).

FINISHED SIZE: 56 x 63in (143 x 160cm)
BLOCK SIZE: 16in

Fun of the Fair 99

Making the Quilt

MAKING THE SQUARE IN A SQUARE UNIT

1 Draw a diagonal line from corner to corner on the wrong side of a 4½in square allocated for the corners of the centre snowball unit (fig 2).

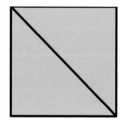

FIG 2

2 With right sides together, lay the marked square on one corner of the 8½in square, aligning the outer edges. Sew across the diagonal, using the marked diagonal line as the stitching line (fig 3).

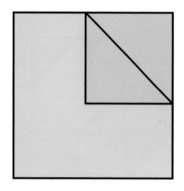

FIG 3

TIP The flip-over corners of this unit could be thought of as a waste of fabric, but they can be re-purposed to make a bonus quilt. After step 2, you can sew a parallel line ½in from the marked diagonal line as shown and then cut between the two sewn lines (fig 4). This is not an integral part of this quilt but it does give you lots of lovely half-square triangle units which you can use to make our bonus quilt, Step Into Spring (see page 108). Do keep your ½in parallel line accurate so your half-square triangles stay accurate. They should measure 3¾in.

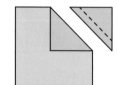

FIG 4

3 Flip the square over and press towards the outside of the block to form a snowball corner. If you have drawn a parallel line, cut between the sewn lines and set the excess aside for our bonus quilt (see page 108). If you have not drawn a parallel line, trim the excess fabric. Repeat on all four corners (fig 5). Press.

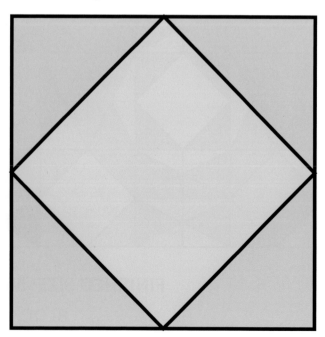

FIG 5

MAKING THE TRIANGLE IN A SQUARE UNIT

4 Take one 4½ x 21in strip allocated for the centre triangle in the triangle in a square unit and lay the centre triangle of the Two Peaks in One ruler on the strip as shown, lining up the 4½in strip line with the bottom of the strip and the cut off top of the triangle at the top of the strip (fig 6). Cut one centre triangle.

5 Rotate the ruler 180° and cut the second centre triangle, lining up the 4½in strip line with the top of the strip and the cut off top of the triangle at the bottom of the strip (fig 7).

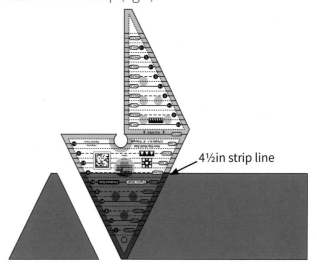

4½in strip line

FIG 7

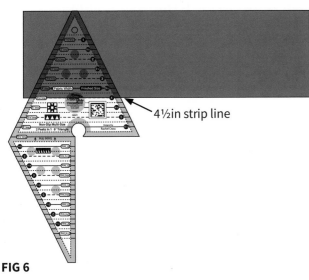

4½in strip line

FIG 6

6 Continue along the strip to cut six centre triangles. Repeat with the second 4½ x 21in strip and cut a further six centre triangles. You can of course layer the two strips and cut both together. You need eight centre triangles for the block so set the others aside for the outer units. You need twenty-eight for the outer units in total.

7 Take one 4½ x 21in strip allocated for the inner side triangles and fold it so that a pair of triangles can be cut at the same time. Lay the side triangle section of the Two Peaks in One ruler on the strip as shown, aligning the 4½in strip line with the bottom of the strip and the cut off top of the triangle at the top of the strip (fig 8). Cut one pair of side triangles.

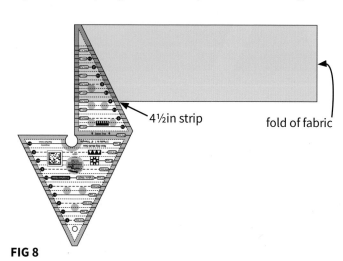
4½in strip fold of fabric

FIG 8

8 Rotate the ruler and cut the second pair of side triangles (fig 9).

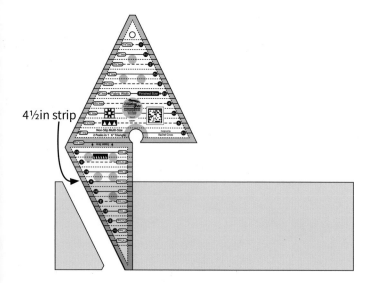
4½in strip

FIG 9

IMPORTANT NOTE Every time you cut a pair of side triangles, move the ruler so that the base line is along the bottom of the triangle. There is a cut off corner on the ruler to use as a guide and use this to nub off the corner (fig 10). It takes a little extra time but it is well worth the effort. We don't always remind you to do this but it will keep your work accurate.

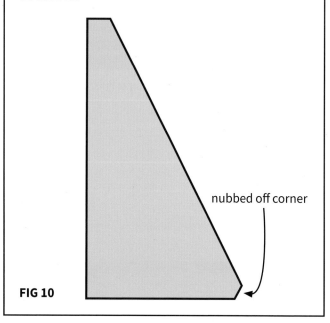
nubbed off corner

FIG 10

9 Continue to make six pairs of side triangles. You need four pairs of side triangles for the block so set aside the additional pairs for the outer blocks (fig 11). You need a total of twenty-eight pairs for the outer blocks.

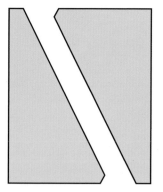

FIG 11

10 Repeat steps 7–9 with the 4½ x 21in strip allocated for the outer side triangles to make four pairs for the block and set additional pairs aside for the outer blocks (fig 12). You need twenty-eight pairs for the outer blocks.

11 Take one centre triangle, one left side triangle in one colour and one right side triangle in the other colour (fig 13).

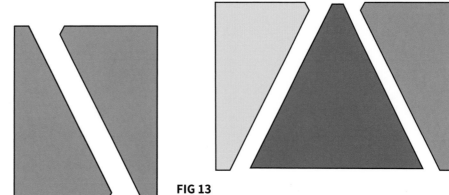

FIG 13

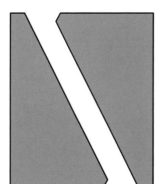

FIG 12

12 Sew the right-hand triangle to the right side of the centre triangle. Press away from the centre triangle (fig 14).

FIG 14

13 Sew a left-hand triangle to the unit and press away from the centre triangle (fig 15). The unit should measure 4½in square. Repeat to make four.

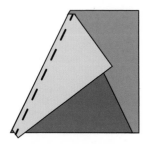

FIG 15

14 Repeat to make another four units with the side triangles reversed (fig 16). You now have eight units.

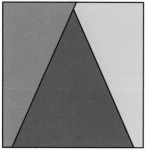

FIG 16

15 Sew one of each unit together as shown (fig 17). Press. We found pressing the remaining seams of the block open worked best for us.

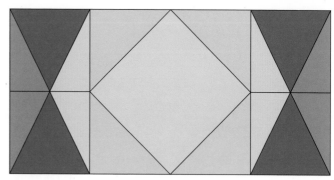

FIG 17

16 Sew two of these units to the left and right of the centre square in a square unit (fig 18) and **STOP!**

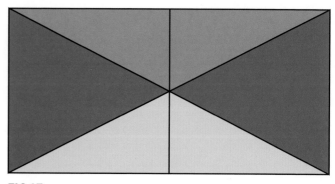

FIG 18

17 Set the units aside keeping them together and repeat steps 1–16 to make twelve blocks (fig 19).

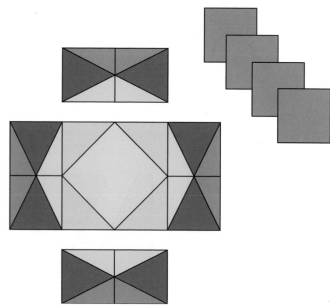

FIG 19

ASSEMBLING THE QUILT

18 From the remaining strips cut thirty-two 4½in squares for the snowball corners of the outer 8½in squares.

19 You may now assemble your quilt and you have:

■ Twelve partially sewn blocks

■ Twenty 8½in squares

■ Thirty-two 4½in squares for the snowball corners of the outer squares

■ Twenty-eight centre triangles for the outer triangle in a square blocks

■ Twenty-eight pairs of side triangles for the outer triangle in a square blocks.

20 Referring to fig 20, lay out your blocks choosing where to place the extra twenty 8½in squares. You will now be able to see where the snowball corners of the blocks have to be sewn. Sew these snowball corners in place making sure they are all in the correct position. It is important to make sure these are all sewn in the correct place before deciding where to position additional snowball corners.

FIG 20

21 Now that the blocks are complete, sew the remaining thirty-two snowball corners in place to complete the square in a square blocks around the outside of the quilt.

22 Using the twenty-eight centre triangles and twenty-eight pairs of side triangles make up twenty-eight triangle in a square units. For these outer units we sewed a right and a left side triangle in the same fabric, but you can make these as varied as you like. Sew two units together as shown and position them around the quilt (fig 21).

23 When you are happy with the layout (and you have double and triple checked everything!), sew the units together in rows and then sew the rows together (fig 22). Press well.

24 Your quilt is complete. Quilt as desired and bind to finish (see *General Techniques*).

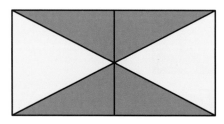

FIG 21

FIG 22

Step into Spring

This is the bonus quilt which you can make using the 128 half-square triangle units from the Fun of the Fair quilt. These half-square triangles measure 3¾in (3¼in finished size).

Preparation

YOU WILL NEED

- 128 3¾in half-square triangle units (3¼in finished)
- 1½ yards (1.4m) background fabric
- ½yd (0.5m) binding fabric, or a scrappy binding can be made from the excess fabric (see tip on page 110)

Starting from Scratch?

If you would like to make this quilt but don't have the ready-sewn half-square triangles, you need to cut 128 assorted 4⅛in squares which amounts to approx. 1.5m (1¾yd). Cut them in half diagonally, mix them up and re-sew the triangles together randomly to make 3¾in half-square triangles (3¼in finished).

FINISHED SIZE: 48 x 57in (122 x 145cm)
BLOCK SIZE: 6½in

This quilt was made from the half-square triangles produced when we made the Fun of the Fair quilt. We never like to see anything wasted! It was made by the authors and quilted by The Quilt Room.

PREPARING THE UNITS

Sew four half-square triangle units together as shown. Press and trim if necessary to measure 7in square (fig 1).

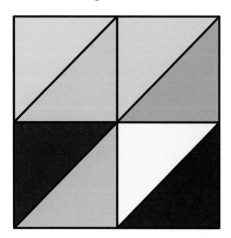

FIG 1

CUTTING THE BACKGROUND FABRIC

■ Cut four 7in strips across the width of the fabric and sub-cut each into five 7in squares. You need twenty in total.

■ Cut two 11½in strips across the width of the fabric and sub-cut into four 11½in squares. Cut across both diagonals of each 11½in square to make a total of sixteen setting triangles (fig 2).

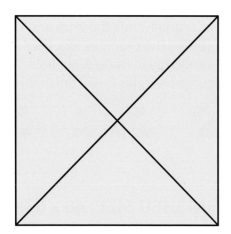

FIG 2

■ Using the excess from the 11½in strips cut two 6½in squares. Cut across one diagonal of each square to make four corner triangles (fig 3). Cutting the setting and corner triangles in this way ensures that there are no bias edges on the outside of your quilt.

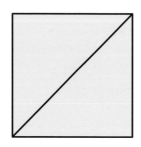

FIG 3

ASSEMBLING THE QUILT

1 Referring to fig 4, lay out your blocks in rows, making sure the blocks are facing the right way as shown. When you are happy with the arrangement, start with row 1 and sew the blocks into rows with a setting triangle at both ends. Don't sew the corner triangles on yet. The setting triangles are cut slightly larger to make the blocks 'float', so when

sewing the setting triangles make sure the bottom of the triangle is aligned with the bottom of the block (fig 5). Press as shown.

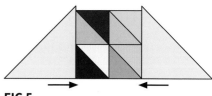

FIG 5

2 Sew the rows together, pinning at every seam intersection to ensure a perfect match. Sew the corner triangles on last. Press well.

3 Your quilt is complete. Quilt as desired and bind to finish (see *General Techniques*).

> **TIP** We made a scrappy binding from the left-over fabrics. Cut into 2½in wide strips and sew into a continuous length measuring approx. 240in.

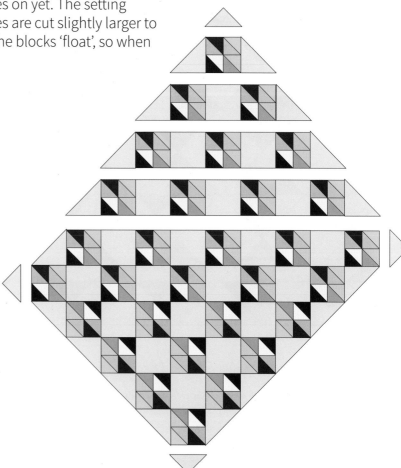

FIG 4

Templates

All these templates can be downloaded from
quiltroom.co.uk/wp-content/uploads/2021/07/QFQtemplates.pdf
Always check that your printer is set to output at 100%, not 'shrink to fit'.

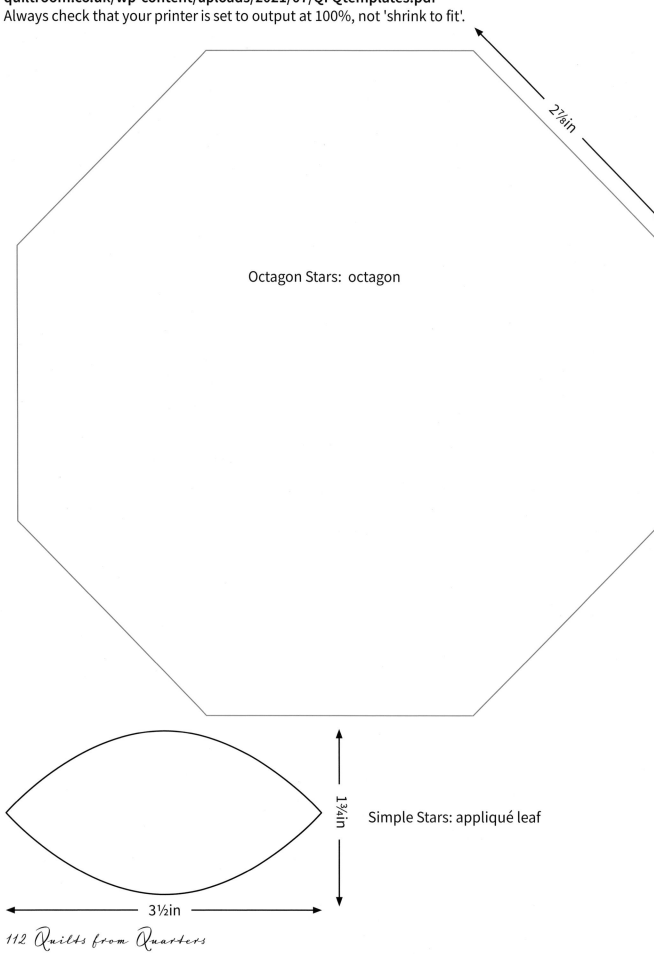

Octagon Stars: octagon

2⅞in

Simple Stars: appliqué leaf

1¾in

3½in

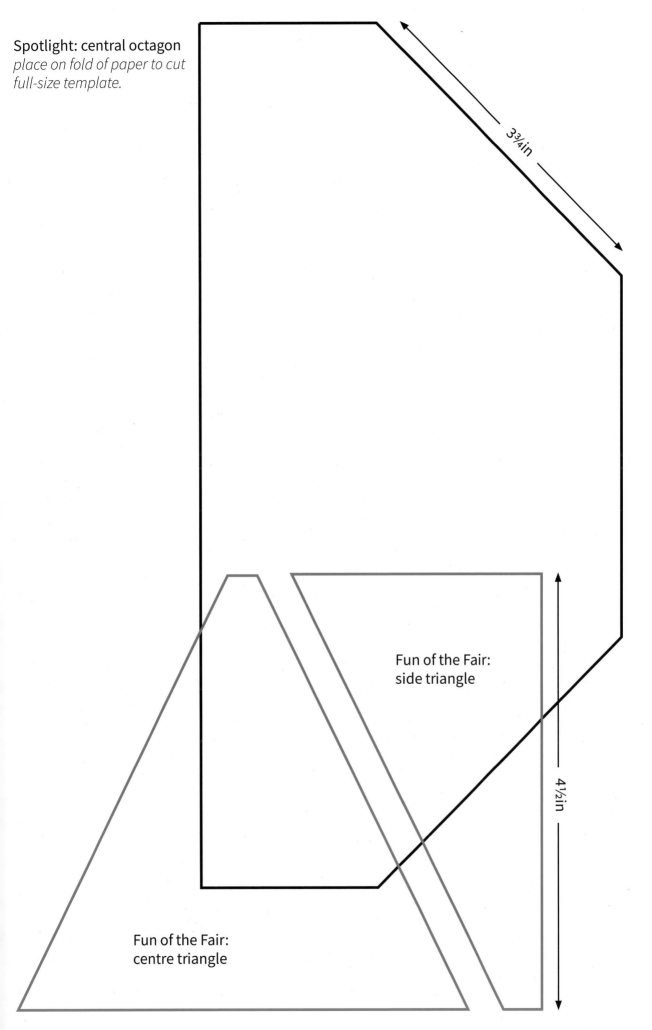

Spotlight: central octagon
place on fold of paper to cut full-size template.

3¾in

Fun of the Fair:
side triangle

4½in

Fun of the Fair:
centre triangle

General Techniques

Tools

All the projects in this book require rotary cutting equipment. You will need a self-healing cutting mat that is at least 18 x 24in, and a rotary cutter.

Any rotary cutting work requires rulers and most people have a make they prefer. We like the Creative Grids rulers as their markings are clear, they do not slip on the fabric and their Turn-a-Round facility is so useful when dealing with half-inch measurements. We recommend the 6½ x 24½in ruler, plus a large square ruler which is handy for squaring up blocks or a finished quilt top, and making sure you are always cutting at right angles.

We also use certain speciality rulers as they make cutting so much speedier and more accurate. In our Spotlight quilt we have used the 90⁰ triangle from the Creative Grids Flying Geese and 45/90 ruler, although you can use a quilting square instead and we give instructions for this in our pattern. In our Diamond Sparkle quilt we've used a 60⁰ triangle, and in Fun of the Fair we've used the Creative Grids Two Peaks in One triangle. There are other brands of rulers you can use but just be sure you are using the correct markings.

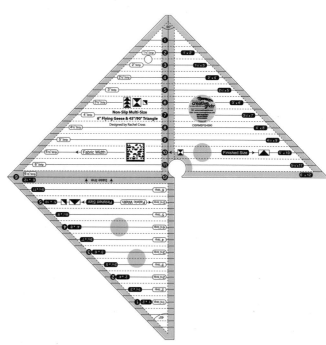

CREATIVE GRIDS FLYING GEESE AND 45/90 TRIANGLE RULER – CGRMSFG4590

CREATIVE GRIDS 2 PEAKS IN 1 RULER – CGR2P1

Seams

We cannot stress enough the importance of maintaining an accurate ¼in seam allowance throughout. We prefer to say an accurate scant ¼in seam because there are two factors to take into consideration. Firstly, the thickness of your thread, and secondly when you press your seam allowance to one side it takes up a tiny amount of fabric. These are both extremely small amounts but if they are ignored you will find your exact ¼in seam allowance isn't quite as exact as you hoped and is in fact taking up more than ¼in.

It is well worth testing your seam allowance before starting on a quilt, and most sewing machines have various needle positions that can be used to make any adjustments.

HOW DO I CHECK MY SEAM ALLOWANCE?

1 Use this simple test. Take a scrap 2½in strip of fabric and cut off three segments, each 1½in wide.

2 Sew two segments together down the longer side and press seam to one side.

3 Sew the third segment across the top. It should fit exactly (fig 1a). If it doesn't, you need to make an adjustment to your seam allowance. If the top segment is too long (fig 1b), your seam allowance is too wide and can be corrected by moving the needle on your sewing machine to the right. If it is too short (fig 1c), your seam allowance is too narrow and this can be corrected by moving the needle to the left.

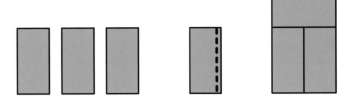

FIG 1A

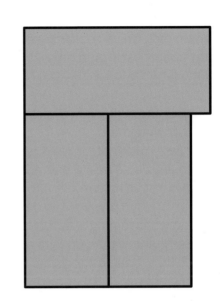

FIG 1B

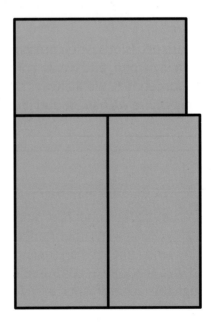

FIG 1C

PRESSING

In quiltmaking, pressing is of vital importance and if extra care is taken you will be well rewarded.

■ Always set your seam after sewing by pressing the seam as sewn, without opening up your strips. This eases any tension and prevents the seam line from distorting.

■ Move the iron with an up and down motion, zigzagging along the seam rather than ironing down the length of it, which could cause distortion.

■ Open up your patchwork and press on the right side of the fabric towards the darker fabric, if necessary guiding the seam underneath to make sure the seam is going in the right direction. Press with an up and down motion.

■ Always take care if using steam and certainly don't use steam anywhere near a bias edge.

■ Unless there is a special reason for not doing so, seams should be pressed towards the darker fabric. The main criteria when joining seams is to have the seam allowances going in the opposite direction to each other as they then nest together without bulk. Your patchwork will lie flat and your seam intersections will be accurate.

> **TIP** There are occasions when pressing the seams open is helpful, and we do consider doing this sometimes. We'll always say in the instructions where we have found it easier to do so.

PINNING

Never underestimate the benefits of pinning. When you have to align a seam it is important to insert pins to stop any movement when sewing. Long, fine pins with flat heads are recommended as they will go through the layers of fabric easily and allow you to sew up to and over them.

Seams should always be pressed in opposite directions so they will nest together nicely. Insert a pin either at right angles or diagonally through the seam intersection ensuring that the seams are matching perfectly. When sewing, do not remove the pin too early as your fabric might shift and your seams will not be perfectly aligned.

Piecing Know How

WHAT IS CHAIN PIECING?

Chain piecing is the technique of feeding a series of pieces through the sewing machine without lifting the presser foot and without cutting the thread between each piece (fig 2). Always chain piece when you can – it saves time and thread. Once your chain is complete simply snip the thread between the pieces.

WHAT DO I DO ABOUT DOG EARS?

A dog ear is the excess piece of fabric which overlaps past the seam allowance when sewing triangles. Dog ears should always be cut off to reduce bulk. They can be trimmed using a rotary cutter although snipping with small sharp scissors is quicker. Make sure you are trimming the points parallel to the straight edge of the triangle (fig 3).

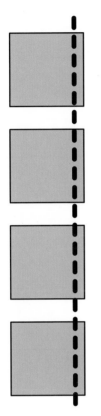

FIG 2

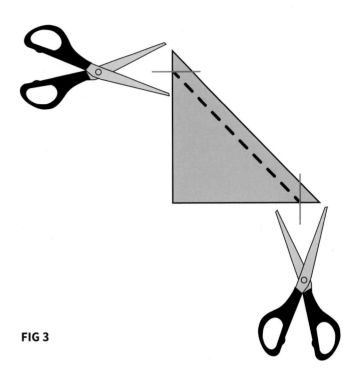

FIG 3

Adding Borders

1   Begin by sewing all your border strips into one continuous length. If you need to join strips for your borders and binding, you may choose to join them with a diagonal seam to make them less noticeable. Press the seams open (fig 4a).

2   Determine the vertical measurement from top to bottom through the centre of your quilt top. Cut two side border strips to this measurement. Mark the halves and quarters of one quilt side and one border with pins. Placing right sides together and matching the pins, stitch the quilt top and border together, easing the quilt side to fit where necessary. Repeat on the opposite side. Press the seams open (fig 4b).

3   Determine the horizontal measurement from side to side across the centre of the quilt top. Cut two top and bottom border strips to this measurement and add to the quilt top in the same manner (fig 4c).

TIP The fabric requirements in this book all assume you are going to be sewing straight rather than mitred borders. If you intend to have mitred borders please add sufficient fabric for this.

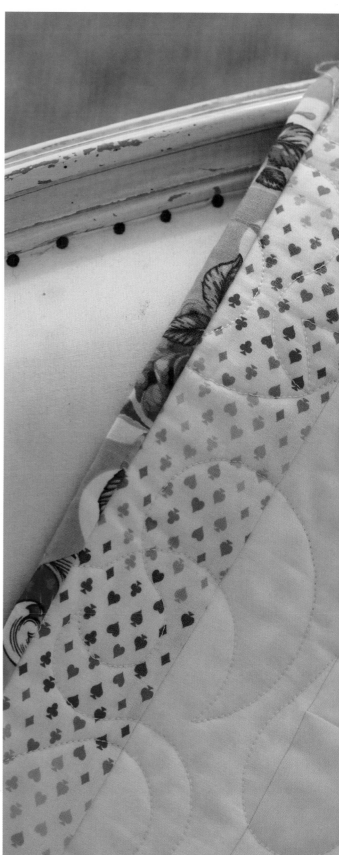

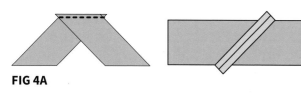

FIG 4A

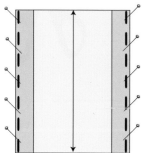

FIG 4B

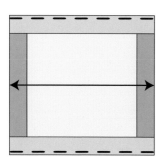

FIG 4C

Setting on Point

The simplest quilt can take on a totally different look when set on point. Square Deal is an example of a quilt set diagonally or 'on point' and the step-by-step instructions contain all the information you need to make that quilt. However, you might like to try one of the other quilts to see what it looks like on point and for this reason we have included information for setting quilts on point. Some people are a little daunted as there are a few points to take into consideration, but here is all you need to know.

HOW WIDE WILL MY BLOCKS BE WHEN SET ON POINT?

To calculate the measurement of the block from point to point you multiply the size of the finished block by 1.414.

Example: a 12in block will measure 12in x 1.414 which is 16.97in – just under 17in.

Now you can calculate how many blocks you need for your quilt.

HOW DO I PIECE BLOCKS ON POINT?

Piece rows diagonally, starting at a corner. Triangles have to be added to the end of each row before joining the rows together and these are called setting triangles.

HOW DO I CALCULATE WHAT SIZE SETTING TRIANGLES TO CUT?

Setting triangles form the outside of your quilt and need to have the straight of grain on the outside edge to prevent stretching. To ensure this, these triangles are formed from quarter square triangles, i.e. a square cut into four. The measurement for this is: diagonal block size + 1¼in

Example: a 12in block (diagonal measurement approx 17in) should be 18¼in.

Corner triangles are added last. They also need to have the outside edge on the straight of grain of the fabric so these should be cut from half square triangles. To calculate the size of square to cut in half, divide the finished size of your block by 1.414 then add ⅞in.

Example: a 12in block would be 12in divided by 1.414 = 8.49in + ⅞in (0.88) = 9.37in (or 9½in as it can be trimmed later).

Most diagonal quilts start off with one block and in each row thereafter the number of blocks increases by two. All rows contain an odd number of blocks. To figure the finished size of the quilt, you count the number of diagonals across and multiply this by the diagonal measurement of the block. Do the same with the number of blocks down and multiply this by the diagonal measurement of the block.

Binding Your Quilt

The fabric requirements in this book are for a 2½in double-fold French binding cut on the straight of grain.

■ Trim the excess backing and wadding so that the edges are even with the top of the quilt.

■ Join your binding strips into a continuous length, making sure there is sufficient to go around the quilt plus 10–12in for the corners and overlapping ends.

■ With wrong sides together, press the binding in half lengthways. Fold and press under ½in to neaten edge at the end where you will start sewing.

■ On the right side of the quilt and starting about 12in away from a corner, align the raw edges of the double thickness binding with the raw edge of the quilt and pin in place. Sew with a ¼in seam allowance, leaving the first inch open.

■ At the first corner, stop ¼in from the edge of the quilt and backstitch. Lift your needle and presser foot. Fold the binding upwards, away from you but in line with the next raw side of the quilt, then fold again this time downwards along the raw quilt side (fig 5). Pin in place. Turn the quilt and stitch from the edge to ¼in from the next corner and repeat the turn.

FIG 5

■ Continue all around the quilt working each corner in the same way. When you come to the starting point, cut the binding, fold under the cut edge and overlap at the starting point.

■ Fold over the binding to the back of the quilt and hand stitch in place, folding the binding at each corner to form a neat mitre.

Backing Fabric

The patterns in this book do not include fabric requirements for backing as many people like to use wide backing fabric so they do not have to have any joins.

■ **Using wide fabric**, it is a simple calculation as to how much you need to buy. For example, if your quilt is 54 x 72in. Your backing needs to be 3–4in larger all round so your backing measurement is 60 x 78in. If you have found 60in wide backing fabric, then you would buy the length, which is 78in. However, if you have found 90in wide backing, you can turn it round and you would only have to buy the width of 60in.

■ **Using 42in wide fabric** you will need to have a join or joins in order to get the required measurement unless the backing measurement for your quilt is 42in or less on one side. If your backing measurement is less than 42in then you need only buy one length.

■ Using the previous example, if your backing measurement is 60 x 78in, you will have to have one seam somewhere in your backing. If you join two lengths of 42in fabric together your new fabric measurement will be 84in (less a little for the seam). This would be sufficient for the length of your quilt so you need to buy two times the width, i.e. 60in x 2 = 120in. Your seam will run horizontally.

■ If your quilt length is more than your new backing fabric measurement of 84in you will need to use the measurement of 84in for the width of your quilt and you will have to buy two times the length. Your seam will then run vertically.

The Quilt Room
40th Anniversary

From ribbons to quilts..

The opening of our quilt shop in West Street, Dorking in 1988, where we were located for over 20 years.

Alongside designing and writing books, Pam and Nicky own The Quilt Room in Dorking, England, which has been in business now for 40 years. A fortieth anniversary is something rather special and certainly a milestone to celebrate. When Pam first opened the shop way back in 1981 there were just two other specialist quilt shops in the whole of the UK. Those quilt shops are unfortunately no longer around and so The Quilt Room is now officially the longest established quilt shop in the UK, which is a huge honour. Nicky was a toddler when The Quilt Room first opened so it is fair to say most of her life has been spent amongst quilts and fabric.

So much has changed and evolved over the last four decades. It seems inconceivable now that when our shop first opened no one had thought of cutting with a rotary cutter! When this technique arrived on the scene it revolutionised the making of patchwork quilts and Pam embraced those speedy rotary cutting and piecing methods. Customers were enthusiastic to learn different innovations and The Quilt Room workshops were always full, with tutors coming from all over the country to stay. What a privilege to get to know so many talented people! In 1992 *The Quilt Room Patchwork & Quilting Workshops* was published followed by *The Quilter's Workbook* in 1993. Then came a book by That Patchwork Place, who were producing a series of books from quilting shops around America, and we were the first shop to be featured in their 'International Series' in 1995.

In 2005, Nicky made the decision to leave paediatric nursing and join The Quilt Room. In late 2006 we bought our first longarm machine from the States: the magnificent Gammill Statler Stitcher, which was the first Statler Stitcher in the UK. Suddenly we were able to make and finish our quilt samples in record speed. Longarm quilting at that time was beginning to pick up pace, and now we have two longarm machines with a huge client base. Our website has also progressed from the simple design we used over fifteen years ago, to our current website – a beautiful and comprehensive online portal to all that The Quilt Room offers, for customers from all over the UK and abroad. We have spent many hours over many years building our website to what it is now, and are hugely proud of it.

There have been so many fun occasions to look back on and

Pam and Rosemary Miller, who came to work at The Quilt Room in 1983 and became Pam's business partner for many happy years.

certainly one of them was sewing the BBC's *Woman's Hour* Quilt in 1993 to celebrate women's suffrage. It went on display at the House of Commons for a week as part of their festival 'Women Into Politics' and then moved to the Victoria & Albert Museum where it is now held.

Another highlight is Quilt Market – the trade show we attend in the States every year – in particular, Spring Market in 2007 which was held in Portland and coincided with the release of our first David & Charles book, *Jelly Roll Quilts*. We had a blast promoting the book with our first 'schoolhouse' and shared many laughs, giggles, and cocktails with other talented quilters there. Quilt Market is such an

The first location of The Quilt Room – a beautiful beamed room dating back to the 15th century.

Pam with the Woman's Hour *Quilt which is now held at the Victoria & Albert Museum.*

inspiring show and is often where we draw a lot of our inspiration – in fact, it was at one of these shows in 2006 that we were gifted our first jelly roll from Moda and were asked what we thought of it. Another year we were told we must bring tuffets back to the UK – and yes, we did!

If there is one thing over the last forty years to be grateful for, then it is our Quilt Room team. Our team is something rather special – the majority are quilters and passionate about fabric. Even those who have worked for us who were not initially quilters have been persuaded to make something! We have had many lovely ladies work for us over the years, some we have now sadly lost. We have shared a few tears together but most of all, huge amounts of love, laughs and support.

Looking around our shop today, the fabrics are eclectic, colourful, and inspiring. Pam remembers that she started the shop with four bolts of fabric – brown, brown, brown and brown – different shades of course but yes, they were all brown! Nicky's love of colour and Pam's love of vintage blend perfectly together and the shelves are a joy to behold – and there's very little brown to see at all...

So, here is to our fortieth anniversary and let there be many more to come!

Our bright and colourful shop today, just outside Dorking.

Acknowledgements

Being able to design and write about what we love is a real privilege. Special thanks to our wonderful husbands, Nick and Rob, who have always given us their continued and oh so valuable support, usually in the form of a glass of wine at the end of a hard day!

Thank you to our loyal Quilt Room team whose support throughout a difficult year in lockdown has kept everything ticking over. Special thanks to Chris, who runs our longarm department and who always take such great care and skill quilting our quilts and sneaking them to the top of the waiting list.

A big thank you to our lovely fabric distributors, Moda, FreeSpirit Fabrics, Tilda's World, Anbo Textiles and Makower UK for supplying us with early fabrics so we could make our quilts in time and thanks to Janome for the loan of their extra special machine – the M7 Continental – wow what an amazing sewing machine!

Lastly, thank you to our wonderful customers. Their unwavering support continues to amaze and humble us.

Addresses

The Quilt Room
01306 877307
quiltroom.co.uk

Creative Grids (UK) Limited
01664 501724
creativegrids.com

Janome UK Ltd.
0161 666 6011
janome.co.uk

Moda Fabrics/United Notions
800-527-9447
modafabrics.com

Anbo Textiles
01494 450155
anbo.co.uk

FreeSpirit Fabrics
866-907-3305
freespiritfabrics.com

Tilda's World
tildasworld.com

Makower UK
01628 509640
makoweruk.com

About the Authors

The love of sewing has always been in the Lintott genes. Pam first opened her quilt shop, The Quilt Room, in September 1981 when Nicky was just a toddler – so the timing of this book is incredibly special as a 40th anniversary in business is one to celebrate! In 2018 Pam and Nicky relocated their shop to the outskirts of Dorking which has the advantage of plenty of parking, plus the longarm machines, mail order and shop are all under one roof. It makes for a happy environment. Nicky runs the day-to-day side of the business and website, allowing Pam more time to sew.

Pam lives in beautiful Cornwall with her husband, three dogs, chickens, guinea fowl and a flock of sheep. Nicky lives in lovely West Sussex with her husband, three small children and step-daughter nearby, and (currently) with no dogs, chickens, guinea fowl or flocks of sheep.

Designing is a huge passion for both Pam and Nicky and being able to inspire other quilters is a real joy. Pam is the author of The Quilt Room Patchwork & Quilting Workshops and The Quilter's Workbook and Pam and Nicky together have written thirteen books for F&W Media on jelly roll quilts and other pre-cuts. Quilts from Quarters is their fourteenth book together. They have also self-published a selection of booklets and patterns. You can keep in touch with Pam and Nicky on Instagram and Facebook @thequiltroom.

A Quilt Room Publications Book
© Pam and Nicky Lintott 2021
www.quiltroom.co.uk

ISBN 978-1-3999-0005-8

Text, Photography and Design © Pam and Nicky Lintott 2021

First published in 2021

Printed in the UK by Brightsea Print Group for
Quilt Room Publications, 7–9 Beare Green Court, Old Horsham Road, Beare Green, Dorking RH5 4QU, UK